To P[...]
with [...]

P[signature]

The management
of myths

To Bronwen, Liam (our own Newfoundlander) and Ivan

The management of myths

The politics of legitimation in a Newfoundland community

ANTHONY P. COHEN

Manchester University Press

© 1975 Manchester University Press

All rights reserved

Published by Manchester University Press
Oxford Road, Manchester M13 9PL

ISBN 0 7190 0601 5

Printed in Great Britain by
John Sherratt & Son Ltd, The St Ann's Press, Altrincham

Contents

			PAGE
		List of tables and figures	vi
		Preface	vii
CHAPTER	ONE	Theoretical themes in the study of Focaltown politics	1
	TWO	The setting	22
	THREE	The myth managers	38
	FOUR	The political objectives of myth management in Focaltown	61
	FIVE	Styles of articulation as strategies of myth management	75
	SIX	Myth management in the production of support	99
	SEVEN	The problem of legitimacy in Focaltown politics: conclusion	115
		Bibliography	132
		Index	142

List of tables and figures

TABLE ONE	Past and present executive membership of policy-making and service organisations in Focaltown PAGE	56
TWO	Positions in poll, percentages of votes, and predominant electorate features, by polling district: Focaltown municipal election, November 1969	78
THREE	Pentecostalist candidates' positions in poll and percentages of votes, by polling district: Focaltown municipal election, November 1969	104
FOUR	Distribution of responses indicating deference to authority as opposed to personal decision	118
FIVE	Distribution of responses attributing motives for public service	119
SIX	Distribution of responses attributing motives to politicians	119
SEVEN	Distribution of responses indicating family and community orientation (i)	124
EIGHT	Distribution of responses indicating family and community orientation (ii)	124
FIGURE ONE	Modes of group articulation	77
TWO	Vehicles of support mobilisation	99

Preface

The research on which this book was based was conducted under a Fellowship of the Institute of Social and Economic Research, Memorial University of Newfoundland, and financed by the Department of Community and Social Development, Government of Newfoundland and Labrador. I am most grateful to both bodies for their support.

In my experience, politics is a highly sensitive matter in rural Newfoundland, to the extent that I fear my informants may be embarrassed by what I have written. I apologise for imposing on them, for I realise that such research could be regarded as an impertinent intrusion into their lives. I am, nevertheless, immensely grateful for the great help they gave me. For obvious reasons, I have disguised the location and identity of the community and of the *dramatis personae* as best I could, within the limits of accurate ethnography. I must thank especially the man who may recognise himself as the Donald Farrar of this book, for his generosity in easing my passage in Focaltown, and for the time he unstintingly made available to me.

A substantial body of data was collected by survey in 1969. Little of it is used here since it was later lost in transit, but I must express my gratitude to those who helped me in its compilation and organisation. Pat Herrick was especially helpful in designing the questionnaire schedule, whilst Paul Duncan, John Shiry, David Swyers and Peter Eddison rendered computable order out of numerical chaos.

Mrs Marjorie Gray most generously found the time and patience to help me produce a legible manuscript. I owe particular thanks to Martin Spencer of Manchester University Press for his kindness and tact.

During the six years which elapsed between the inception of fieldwork and the completion of this book, many colleagues assisted me, in numerous ways. Clinton Herrick and Fred Evans were most generous with their encouragement and active assistance during the fieldwork. My approach to the various issues reported here owes much to my collaboration at various times with George Perlin, Cato Wadel and, especially, John L. Comaroff. They also read and criticised early drafts of parts or all of this book, as did Ioan Davies, Roy Fitzhenry, Julius Gould, Clinton Herrick,

Dilys Hill, Ralph Matthews, Tom Nemec, Basil Sansom, John Smith, Robert Stebbins and Geoffrey Stiles.

I must make special acknowledgement to Robert Paine and Peter Worsley who have guided me with tolerance, incisive and constructive criticism, and example. The present form of this book has been substantially shaped by the painstaking thoroughness with which they read and criticised the penultimate draft. I am uneasily aware that the final product will satisfy neither of them.

My greatest debt is to my wife, Bronwen Cohen, whose help at every stage of this project has been invaluable. Without her vigilant criticism, uninhibited frankness, and constant encouragement I should have given up long ago.

Manchester, 1974

CHAPTER ONE

Theoretical themes in the study of Focaltown politics

INTRODUCTION

This study is concerned with the ways in which two groups of leaders in Focaltown,[1] a Newfoundland community, compete for legitimacy. It describes the groups' characteristic strategies of legitimisation as exercises in the management of political myths and, in so doing, it treats legitimacy as a scarce and valued resource which structures the political relationship between the two groups. The study is set within the historical context of rapid change in Newfoundland society, and of the traumatic processes of acculturation and cultural adaptation which have attended the province's growing incorporation into the social life of the North American mainland. It is precisely this situation of instability and cultural crisis which has rendered problematic the legitimacy of activists in community leadership, for change has brought into question the values with which leaders traditionally sustained themselves, and the new structures of leadership have not stabilised sufficiently to allow appropriate 'supportive' values to emerge. In periods of stability, a leader pursues legitimacy by demonstrating his association with those 'sacralised' values which define legitimate leadership, but the competing activists with whom I deal are seeking to promote definitions of what those values should be.

The study thus constitutes an initial statement in a developing approach to political phenomena, in which politics is associated paradigmatically (though not definitionally) with the control of cognition and with the management of those meanings which actors perceive in relations of inequality. The present monograph focuses upon the employment by leadership activists of mythic devices to persuade an audience that they conform to the principles which constitute a salient definition of legitimate leadership. It thus describes the strategies of presentation adopted by these leaders to induce in the audience the perception of themselves *as legitimate*.

The ethnography concentrates upon the leaders, upon the ways in which they perceive their own political situations and in which they accordingly plan their behaviour. It largely takes for granted or, at least, does not elaborate on the values and practices which typically constitute the political culture of non-activist Focaltowners.

2 The management of myths

THEORIES OF THE STRUCTURAL DETERMINATION OF POLITICAL LEGITIMACY

The politics of leadership in Focaltown is about legitimacy. Indeed, I argue that legitimacy is the valued and scarce resource which, to a great extent, actually structures political relations in the community. Such an argument deviates rather dramatically from the conventional models of politics to be found in the literature of comparative sociology. In these models, the association between political behaviour—generally, the incumbency of, what are treated as, political roles—and legitimacy, is reduced to a matter of definition. The nature of the models renders politics legitimate by definition. Thus, empirical processes of legitimisation tend to be described in terms logically implied by *a priori* definitions of politics. By contrast with this, the present study attempts to ground the account of legitimisation in Focaltown in the circumstances of empirical social process, rather than in such axiomatic formulae. I am, therefore, bound to bring these earlier approaches into question.

The accounts they have produced of legitimisation have tended to be of a process *determined* by the structural characteristics of politics as a processually discrete or institutionally circumscribed form of behaviour. These views of politics have produced a succession of taxonomies which sought to classify in universalistic and diacritical terms the features and functions of the political aspects of society, and thus to distinguish these, by definition, from other 'functional' social processes. Hence, in their attempts to suggest what politics is, writers have typically been led to specify structural configurations as being peculiarly 'political'. That is, they have, by definition, identified certain bits of the social structure as being *political*, rather than something else. What has tended to result is the universalistic definition of politics—and, with it, legitimisation—in terms of specific structural referents and loci.

Invariably, the diacritic of politics in these accounts rested on the notion of some specific *function* and, as with all functionalism, the consequent analyses have treated political behaviour and process as structurally determined. This, together with the universalism of the definitions, has meant that such studies have taken little or no account of the empirical and interactional circumstances in which the given 'political' phenomenon is located. They have been identified by definition rather than by observation, and the definitions themselves have been drawn from the logic of their theoretical paradigms, rather than from the data they are supposed to describe.

This practice of 'definition by fiat' has been roundly condemned in sociology (see, e.g., Cicourel, 1964; Glaser and Strauss, 1967), but the criticism has rarely penetrated the sub-fields of political studies. Perhaps this is because political theorists have been known to stigmatise such qualitative methodological issues as being prejudicial to the development of political theory (Easton, 1966, 4). Nevertheless, I would argue that the criticism is no less valid for political studies than for any other branch of comparative sociology, and I associate myself firmly with the recent trend in political anthropology which has sought for ways to ground concepts of political phenomena more securely in the circumstances of empirical social process.

This trend began, perhaps, as a reaction to Radcliffe-Brown's contention (1940) that there are societies which do not have politics. He argued that politics, as a '... special class of social phenomena', should be imputed only to societies displaying the elements of state organisation. Accordingly, he defines politics in terms, reminiscent of Weber, which suggest a state-like organisation for the functional management of conflict and the reassertion of communal legal norms through the sanction of the legitimate use of force (*ibid.*, xiv ff.). In this approach, one may see clearly the delineation of a specific and discrete functional area of the social structure as the special preserve of politics; and, moreover, the notion that political action is essentially collective, performed on behalf of the 'community' as a whole (*loc. cit.*; also Radcliffe-Brown, 1952, 211). Historically, criticism of Radcliffe-Brown's argument began in the very volume of papers to which his essay was a Preface. In their Introduction, Fortes and Evans-Pritchard accept the principal referents of Radcliffe-Brown's definition, but depart from its strict letter, arguing that politics can appear in stateless societies, although in a qualitatively different form. They see such societies as being composites of 'segmentary lineage' systems. They speak of these societies not as lacking *politics*, but as lacking 'government' (Fortes and Evans-Pritchard, 1940, 5). They allow politics to segmentary lineages on the grounds that they are corporate groups. As constituent parts of a wider society, they conduct 'external relations' with the other constituents. Their approach thus attributes to lineage groups the same notion of collectivity or corporateness that constitutes one of Radcliffe-Brown's criteria of politics as a defining characteristic of the state.[2] This emphasis on the function of politics as a means whereby the coherence and unity of the collectivity is maintained appears throughout this seminal book[3] and, indeed, informs what might be called the 'structural-functionalist' school of political analysis.

In this tradition, politics is essentially regarded as the means by which the inherent disorder of human association is mitigated and its unnatural, but *social* contrary—order—is maintained. This is the familiar Hobbesian view which permeates the Durkheimian tradition in structural functionalism and finds exhaustive statement in the work of Talcott Parsons. In these various discussions, politics is seen as the source of the legitimate use of force in 'social control'; but second and, perhaps, more important, it is regarded as those processes by which conflicting or plural interests coalesce to form a consensual equilibrium. The very notion of equilibrium, of course, presupposes prior disorder (cf. Gluckman, 1965, 279–80; also Nadel, 1951, 343; Homans, 1951, 301). But whilst it is axiomatic that the survival of societies is contingent on their capacity to minimise internal strain and entropy, it can only be an arbitrary and definitional truth—and one which offends colloquial usage—to assert that politics is always the means by which this is achieved.

Indeed, the move away from the view of politics as an institutional morphology which maintains unity was informed by the realisation that political action is not only generated by, but frequently generative of *dis*harmony. The significance of such a view is not merely its denial of the inevitability of an equilibrating consensus; it also suggests that politics appears *within* groups, as well as between them. This is the direction in which M. G. Smith sought to argue in his critical refinement of theory on segmentary lineage systems (1956). Smith maintains that politics should be treated as a system of action. It is, he says, that constituent process of government through which actors compete 'in power' to influence decisions of policy (*ibid.*, 47 ff.). He thus repudiates the previous distinctions between societies said to possess and to lack government. Further, he definitionally demolishes the distinction between segmentary and corporate societies: all societies have government; all government has politics; all politics is competitive (or 'contrapositional') and, therefore, all political relationships are segmentary (*ibid.*, 48).

But whilst Smith's avowed intention is to allow politics to *intra*-group relations (*ibid.*, 76), the terms of his definition prevent this. Politics, he says, is a constituent process of *government*, and government is defined as being concerned with 'the *public* affairs of a people' (*ibid.*, 47, my emphasis; see also Smith, 1960, 15), a suggestion which recalls Evans-Pritchard's view of politics as the structural relationship *between* groups or 'political units'. The definition still prevents us from regarding the competitive relationship of A and B as being *intrinsically* political, and thus leaves us with similarly universalistic structural referents for 'politics' as those stipulated in the previous definitions.

There are other universalistic elements in Smith's definition with which the attempt to build a grounded theory of politics might take issue—the stipulation of the essentially competitive nature of politics and the inextricable association between power and governmental structure—but the issues discussed above serve to illustrate the main point I wish to make. Whilst the course of the debate from Radcliffe-Brown to Smith takes us from a wholly structural to an incipiently processual approach, it does not relieve 'politics' of either the inherent defects and constraints of universalistic structural definition or the limitations of a definition in terms of jural role systems or macro-social 'public' affairs.

In all three of these seminal statements politics is given a discrete institutional setting and specific structural features and functions. These things are held to provide the necessary elements a situation must possess if it may be said to be political. Those defining characteristics also stipulate the nature of the association between politics and legitimacy in similarly *a priori* terms. Indeed, legitimacy is treated as a defining characteristic of politics—that is, as a property which is structurally determined by virtue of its location in one functional segment of the social structure rather than another. In the study of Focaltown politics which follows, it will be clear that these referents of 'politics' are not appropriate. Further, it is the central argument of the study that far from being a *given* and diacritical feature of politics, legitimacy is a highly diffuse resource, and one whose salience and unequal distribution may structure political relations.

The structural determinist position is pursued to its fullest logical extent in the work of Parsons and Easton. Here, though in different ways, the definitional association between politics (as a functional 'subsystem' of society) and legitimacy is held to rest on the consensus which is achieved and maintained by the *normally* functioning social system. Though also present in the work of the writers discussed above, it is through the elaborate schemes of Parsons and Easton that one may see most clearly the essential deficiency of the structural-functionalist accounts of politics. The axiomatic associations they stipulate among politics, legitimacy and consensus lead to an account of legitimacy as being politically unproblematic.

Like Radcliffe-Brown and Evans-Pritchard, Parsons stipulates the 'collectivity' as the level of political action (see especially Parsons, 1966*b*, 93; 1960*a*, 181). To the polity he attributes the function of enabling collective decisions to be made and implemented, decisions which, because of their essentially collective orientation, he speaks of—echoing Smith— as being 'affected with a public interest' (*ibid.*, 183; also 1969, 475). Functional demands appear in society which create 'tension' and whose satisfaction is the task of the polity. It is precisely this 'collective system goal-attainment' which Parsons defines as 'political' (*ibid.*, 474). The importance of the structural-functionalist postulate of consensus is evident, firstly in the definitional association of politics with *collective* decisions, and secondly, in the function postulated for the polity of mitigating entropic strain and, thereby, preserving order. The two are, of course, related by their implication of a communality of value in the normally functioning society (cf. Parsons, 1966*a*, 253; and see Sharrock, 1970, 390). If deviation from this occurs its source must, by definition, be sought in some area other than the polity (cf. Mitchell, 1967, 43; Dahrendorf, 1958). Since deviation cannot be regarded as politically generated conflict, there can be no suggestion of a conflict of political values, and one may therefore assert consensus.[4] But Parsons' characterisation of the polity suggests that it preserves and protects the consensus; it leaves the *evolution* of such consensus unexplained. By definition it excludes conflict from political behaviour.

The consensus of which Parsonian sociology speaks is, among other things, an agreement about basic social rules, and is evidenced by the absence of conflict. But, following from the argument outlined above, politics—in Parsons' model—must be seen as being *predicated* on such rules. Like Hobbes and Weber before him, Parsons thus sees the consensus (expressed in terms of collective goals) as giving rise to social rules which are then enforced and maintained through political activity (cf. Parsons, 1960a, 190–1).[5] The implication of this position is that, pursuing Parsons' logic, one is precluded from seeing these rules as the *consequence* of political activity. Just as he leaves unexplained the evolution of consensus, so also he definitionally excludes from the 'political' the creation or generation of rules.[6]

The point at issue here is that of the nature of the relationship between politics and legitimacy. In Parsons' view, politics proceeds from an agreement on social rules and is, therefore, *by definition* legitimate. In other words, it treats legitimacy as a totally unproblematic property of political behaviour.[7] By contrast I would argue that a model of politics must be applicable to the very processes through which rules are formulated and thus, also, through which legitimacy is obtained. My quarrel with Parsons is not merely a semantic one; I contend that the customary meanings of 'politics' are offended if it is not recognised to be largely concerned with the struggle for legitimacy. It is with just such a struggle that this book is concerned. I would suggest that Parsons' peculiarly unpolitical view of politics is a consequence of the logic of the functionalist paradigm, for this leads him to assert the legitimacy of action provided only that it is performed within its 'own' functional subsystem. Quite apart from the circularity of the argument thus implied,[8] it seems to me to stand at odds with empirical political process. The structural determinist view which Parsons enunciates suggests that politics is legitimate by definition and that, therefore, behaviour—such as the exercise of power—which is consensually and collectively classified as political thereby acquires legitimacy. By contrast, the study of leadership in Focaltown suggests that politics is at least as much concerned with the *creation* of legitimacy as with action performed under its prior bestowal: politicians try to create legitimacy for themselves and, *pace* Weber, Parsons and Easton, who see power strictly limited by its legitimacy, they use their power in the attempt. That is to say that power is not given simply by the fact of its legitimacy: it can be used to create legitimacy. This eventuality is not described by Parsons' account of political process.

Neither is it permitted by Easton's elaborate model of the political system. Easton is a key figure in the debate about the definition of politics, for he has an explicit concern to link the traditions of macro and micro-political studies, manifest in his attempt to render the comparative data of the functionalist anthropologists into a coherent theoretical form which, he claims, they have previously lacked (Easton, 1959). His is, also, the last major attempt to set down rigid and universalistic criteria for the definition of social behaviour as political in terms of a 'grand theory'. On both counts, his influence on subsequent writers has been considerable.

For Easton, politics is concerned with '... the authoritative allocation of values for a society'. The allocation is 'authoritative' because members of the system feel themselves to be 'bound' by it (1965a, 50). This clearly recalls Parsons' account of the legitimacy of the political system as deriving from the reciprocal obligations of the collectivity and those it places in authority. The first difficulty with Easton's definition is this stipulation that political action is binding on its participants. The second is its arbitrariness. He recognises that authoritative allocations of value are made in many disparate institutional and interactional spheres within a society. But he does not admit these to the category of the political; instead, he calls them 'parapolitical systems'. He reserves the 'political' to the macro-societal level, at which authoritative allocations are made 'for society' rather than for a smaller, sub-societal entity (1957, 383; 1965a, 50; 1965b, 21). This leads to a third difficulty which lies in the implication that politics is, essentially, uni-directional behaviour as the allocation of values *by* authorities *to* contending parties. Such uni-dimensionality is made explicit by Easton's exclusion from the political system of *non*-authoritative roles—or the sources of 'demands' and 'support'. These are conceptualised as being only 'inputs' into the system (1965a, 110, 112; 1965b, 30, 32).[9] This grossly one-sided view of politics is clearly associated with the structural determinism which characterises the tradition we have been discussing.

All three of these features may be seen to derive, again, from the logically determined notion of the essential legitimacy of politics. Like those of Weber, Radcliffe-Brown and Parsons, Easton's model distinguishes the 'political' system from others by the definitional assertion that it is endowed with legitimacy. Like Parsons, Easton appears to remove from the sphere of the political the *generation* of legitimate power and its subsequent distribution to the 'authorities'.[10] Indeed his definition suggests that this distribution is the *precondition* of politics. I have already argued the desirability of seeing the processes involved in the distribution of power and legitimacy as *intrinsically* political. But further, if we accept Easton's view that the concern of politics is the allocation of values, then there would seem to be no good reason to exclude power and legitimacy from consideration as valued entities in themselves. That, of course, is to suggest that the object of much of political process *is* the generation and distribution of power and legitimacy—and, indeed, those are the very processes with which this book is concerned.

TOWARDS A PROCESSUAL ACCOUNT OF POLITICAL LEGITIMACY

Subsequent attempts in political anthropology to formulate more satisfactory models of politics were largely stimulated by Easton's critique of its earlier efforts (Easton, 1959). Anthropologists' reactions to Easton have been many and varied, ranging from the wholesale adoption of his theoretical schema (e.g. Kuper, 1970) to its outright rejection (A. Cohen 1969). Perhaps the more fruitful arguments were those which, recognising —if only to some limited degree—the diffuseness and diversity of politics in social life, logically realised that Easton might be offering a useful account of certain kinds of political behaviour, but objected either to its partiality (Bailey, 1968) or to its functionalism and reiteration of previous theoretical perspectives (Asad, 1970). Yet the debate continues to produce definitions of politics in terms of particularistic and exclusive referents, definitions which still largely tie politics to notions of government—as either consensual or conflictual domination—or to issues of 'public' concern. Only recently has the debate occasionally proceeded to the assertion, made in the present study, that politics may be manifest in such diverse phenomenal varieties that the possibility of its definition and delineation in specific structural terms is remote. By and large it still seems to be informed by the assumption of the essential distinctiveness of political phenomena—as either behavioural activity or subsocietal entity —which underpins Easton's concern when he asks, 'What activity is *specifically* political?' (1959, 214).

If, however, most of these substantive definitions have failed the test of inclusiveness and empirical sensitivity, they have at least been cast less as absolute statements about what politics actually is, and more as speculative hypotheses about how politics might usefully be explicated. It is precisely this distinction between the 'heuristic model' and the 'account of reality' for which Leach argues in *Political Systems of Highland Burma* (1970 edition, 7–8 and *passim*). Yet it becomes apparent in his own book, as in the work of later writers, that this distinction is an extremely difficult one to maintain: the 'as if' model invariably becomes an account of reality.[11] Even though it is intended to be hypothetical rather than factual, its logic must inevitably exclude many kinds and varieties of phenomena, and must similarly define the phenomena to be included in it. The sociological model employed to order data in conformity with an hypothetical logic invariably confirms the hypothesis.

Nevertheless, the attempt to make the distinction was important, for it served to shift emphasis from the definition of politics as a discrete empirical *type* of social behaviour to a view of politics as merely a conceptual aspect or dimension of more general processes of social interaction. Thus, the use of heuristic models coincided with the attempt to explain political interaction not in terms of the distinctiveness for which the earlier writers had sought, but by making reference to the same generic models used to explain other aspects of interaction process. Thus, for example, Barth applies the notion of transaction to the explanation of leadership (1965; 1966); Blau (1964) elaborates a theory of politics in terms of exchange. We find politics spoken of in terms of conflict (Turner, 1957), games (Bailey, 1969), and a variety of functional processes based on different models of social relations (e.g. Fallers,

1963; Barnes, 1969; Epstein, 1968; Kuper, 1970; A. Cohen, 1969).

The heuristic model must be recognised to be stipulative, since it imputes *a priori* a particular character to empirical phenomena (see Murphy, 1972, 73, n. 3; also Catton, 1966, 317). As such, the substantive definitions of politics which have emerged from these models have tended to treat the association between politics and legitimacy, and the process of legitimisation, as matters of definition. In so doing, they have severely limited the extent to which the ethnography of political phenomena has broken free of previously formulated and logically irrefutable hypotheses (cf. Nettler, 1970, 28).

The analogic and heuristic models have, though, been succeeded by the growing realisation that the axiomatic distinction between political behaviour and social action in general leads only to what Worsley calls 'a logical chain of false deductions' (1973, 220). Anthropologists have thus begun working towards conceptualisations of politics which can accommodate the processual diffuseness implied in the suggestion that politics should be regarded as a dimension of all social interaction. Swartz, Turner and Tuden (1966) and Swartz (1968), for example, suggest the notion of a 'field' of political behaviour, though they subsequently revert to definitions built upon the familiar tenets of functionalism (cf. Asad, 1970, 8). More successfully, Balandier (1970) assimilates social process to a model of political economy in which politics serves to regulate the inequalities inherent in systems of social order; whilst Worsley (1964, 1973) sees politics, at its most general, as the processes by which actors impose their wills upon others.

The struggle for legitimacy among the Focaltown leaders suggests that politics is best seen as an amalgam of the two latter models. Legitimacy is an unequally distributed value, the pursuit of which structures relations between the contending leaders, and between the leaders and their respective groups of followers. At the same time it is valued because it is regarded as enhancing the power of the leaders in question. They use their power to create legitimacy for themselves and, if successful, may find themselves more powerful.[12] However, theirs is not so much a competition for power as for the justification of their respective ideological and cultural positions, and in such a competition, legitimacy has an intrinsic value. Legitimacy is, in this sense, a political resource which is made salient by the peculiar social and historical circumstances of community process in Focaltown at the time of this study. But, similarly, one may identify in any situation of the exercise of power the resource in which power resides. It might be status, sex, money, personality, partisan affiliation, being the boss's son-in-law—an infinity of possible variables whose salience will be determined by the particular interactional situation in question. Power may be seen to consist in the valued resource which, being unequally distributed, gives rise to the 'political' relation. It is precisely this variability according to the circumstances of interaction which renders misleading the attempt to define politics—and, thus, legitimisation—in universalistic, structural terms.

There is a further reason for seeing politics as diffuse and complex behaviour. When actors look at social behaviour from the 'outside', they tend to reduce the situation to the minimal number of factors and variables which makes it intelligible to them. They tend to take little or no account of the profusion of less obvious variables which affect the outcome of any situation. Thus if we want to account for the Prime Minister's frown, we refer to the meetings he held that morning or to some phenomenon which we *typically* associate with Prime Ministerhood, rather than to the possibility that he had just had an argument with some member of his family. To explain why X voted for a particular party, we may refer to class, ethnicity, religion, occupation and so on, but would be unlikely to consider the possibility that he voted one way because a neighbour whom he dislikes voted the other. Yet these neglected variables are crucial and must be encompassed within the explanation of political behaviour.[13] They are, perhaps, best thought of as *local* variables, and their incorporation into the observation and description of political behaviour is the real competence of micro-political studies. Politics at any societal level can be viewed thus microscopically, when acknowledgement is made of the complex variety of values and interactions which inform process among a group of actors. This is to suggest again that it is the nature and content of the situation itself, rather than the *a priori* terms of a definition, which should determine what is to be invested analytically with political significance.

The essence of this argument, opposed as it is to the structural-determinist models discussed above, is that in order to comprehend the politics of any situation, we have to recognise that its relations are not simply given by various structural configurations, but also by a dynamic dimension of culture comprised of the actors' definitions of their situations, their perceptions of the structural contexts of their interactions, the values that they bring to bear on social behaviour. In effect, I am suggesting that we apply to the study of politics the same precepts that interactionist sociologists have for long applied to other aspects of behaviour; namely, the view that the structural context of interaction is mediated as a conditioning force by the interaction itself. We cannot, then, accept the determinist postulate that resources are distributed simply according to a preordained structural logic—the view that political resources inhere in roles and statuses. Rather, the distribution of such resources should be regarded as contingent also upon the strategic potentialities of the participating actors.[14] Indeed, the very *value* of the resources is often contingent upon the interaction. To take an example from the politics literature, the determinist argument has generally seen power as consisting in exclusive structural properties which are held to underlie the supremacy of A over B.[15] But the interactional nature of power is ignored here. Power is only power if it is recognised and valued as such. Thus the power of A's power is not intrinsic, but is contingent upon B's perception of it. Indeed, A's exercise of power may well be dependent on B's *manifest* perception. Further, B's manifest perception does not necessarily indicate the *reality* of A's power: A may simply have given the impression of possessing some power resource or, alternatively, B may be pretending to succumb. At the very least, we may conclude firstly that power consists not only in some structural resource, but also in the resource of management; secondly, that the power of actors must always be thought of as being possibly contingent, and never as being absolute (cf. Gouldner, 1960, 164; also see Worsley, 1964, 20).

Politics is concerned with precisely the interactional behaviour I refer to above. It is essentially behaviour associated with the creation, maintenance or change of systems of unequally distributed, valued social resources. I would regard such behaviour as political, regardless of the ostensible institutional contexts in which it appears. In the Focaltown case described here, legitimacy is the resource to which actors seek to give value, and whose distribution they seek to influence to their own advantage. There is, therefore, no essential association between political behaviour and legitimacy. Indeed, it is the very absence of such an association which provides the rationale for the political struggles of Focaltown's leaders, for these are essentially struggles for legitimacy as a valued and unequally distributed resource.[16]

But whilst legitimacy, as a political phenomenon, is not adequately explained by the logic of definition, it is an invariable *empirical* concern of political behaviour. Legitimisation is both the attribution of value to a resource and the justification of its distribution. It is, therefore, a process enjoined by political relations, structured as they are by unequally distributed and valued social resources.[17]

MYTH AS A MODEL OF POLITICAL LEGITIMISATION

I have suggested that legitimacy is less important to the contending groups of Focaltown leaders as a means of increasing their power than as the justification of the ideological and cultural values expressed in their leadership styles. Neither group seeks a redistribution of power within the community generally, since both of them are sustained by the elitist nature of local leadership. Each privately acknowledges the existence of, and disclaims any interest in, the other's sphere of influence. The essence of their quarrel is concerned more with the efficacy and relevance of their respective strategies and their credentials for leadership in the particular social and historical circumstances of contemporary Focaltown. But these issues of apparent expediency have become elaborated to the extent that they appear as a clash of cultures: the argument is thus conducted as a struggle by each group to have the integrity of its values affirmed.

It is in this sense that legitimacy is the prize with intrinsic value.

Thus, whilst the confrontation is most evident in the contrast of strategies employed by each group, the problem of legitimacy for the leaders is by no means a mere tactical concern. Firstly, the effects of Confederation have wrought fundemental and pervasive change in the culture and organisation of community life in Focaltown. In so doing, they have called into question the customary ideological and structural bases of local leadership. The values which constituted legitimate leadership and which remained essentially unchanged for so long have thus to be redefined in the light of contemporary circumstances.

But, secondly, these very changes have rendered the community increasingly heterogeneous and in the process have emphasised its divisions. In their pursuit of legitimacy, the leaders have turned the points of division into interests which they have then imputed to their respective followers whom they have thereby transformed from mere audiences into constituencies. They have then used these interests as their programmes and credentials for leadership. Thus, through the struggle for legitimacy, the leaders have created niches for themselves; the legitimisation which was made imperative by the processes of social change has now become the very rationale for their behaviour as leaders.

The present book describes some of the ways in which these leaders attempt to accomplish their legitimisation, and suggests that the strategies they employ resemble the functional characters which anthropologists have attributed to myth.[18] I thus refer to these strategies as processes of 'myth management'.

In so far as it is a *political* process, legitimisation is concerned with the unequal distribution of values: it is the attribution of value to a resource, and the justification of its distribution. Political interactants, whose relation is structured by the unequal distribution of some resource, generally behave differently. The greater possession of a valued resource allows licence to behave in ways denied to the lesser. We might therefore say that the legitimation of such a state of affairs consists in a body of principles which is implicitly or explicitly associated with the unequally distributed value. For example, A is a general; B is a lieutenant, and accepting the obligations associated with rank, he must salute first: the legitimation is drawn from the principles which express the value of rank. These principles really constitute bodies of social doctrine which validate forms of behaviour and prescribe values. It is such doctrine that I take to be referred to by the term 'myth'.

It is beyond my purpose and competence to engage in discussion about the meaning and contruction of myths. My concern here is simply to relate certain selected functions of myth to the political process of legitimisation. I do not propose a unique or universalistic function for myth. Indeed, I am inclined to accept the view that myth has a multiplicity of functions (P. Cohen, 1969, 351). Rather, I would simply select from the functions that have been attributed to myth those which have the most analogical relevance to myth-management in Focaltown. Those to which I would draw attention are categorised by Kirk (1970, 254) as being (*a*) 'operative, interative, and validatory', and (*b*) 'speculative and explanatory'. Myths of the former category emphasise the continuity of society and its organisational features, seek historical precedents (or 'charters') for behaviour, and provide emotional support for attitudes and beliefs; generally, they form part of the process of 'binding the volatile present to the traditionally and divinely sanctioned regularity of the past' (*ibid.*, 258). Myths of the second category are generally used to reconcile society to inevitable truths, and to resolve or render tolerable the contradictions which appear in social life. The former category appears in sociology of primarily functionalist and Durkheimian traditions, stressing the solidary nature of society. The second functional type is associated more with dialectical social theory.

Malinowski is, of course, the seminal figure in the first of these traditions. In his view myth serves as a 'charter' for social action, investing action of the present with the sacrality of historical precedent. It thereby legitimates the present in terms of the past[19] and serves the function—which Durkheim attributes to ritual—of reaffirming the underlying principles of social organisation (Malinowski, 1928, 739; 1963*a*, 249–50).

Speaking in the dialectical tradition, Levi-Strauss suggests that one of the prime functions of myth is to reconcile apparent oppositions in social life (e.g. 1965, 99). It is a means by which men make use of elements in their sociocultural experience to mediate the contradictions with which social life confronts them (1966). In this respect, he is proposing a function which complements rather than supplants Malinowski's, for the resolution of cognitive and evaluative tensions deriving from social practices may be expected to have the effect of reinforcing or sustaining those practices. Indeed, it has been argued that Levi-Strauss accepts Malinowski's postulate of a charter function for myth (Leach, 1968, xvii). The complementarity of these 'functions' is illustrated by Devons' conception of the political uses of myth. He suggests that there are inconsistencies throughout social reality between the normative ideals and principles of social organisation and actual behaviour (1956). But whilst these ideals may be continuously transgressed in actuality, we constantly reaffirm them. In so doing the inconsistency is resolved and the 'charter' principle of social organisation is thereby renewed and reinforced.

But there are other mythic processes through which the effects of a contradiction between ideal and practice can be mitigated. Percy Cohen, for example, talks of myth as being a device 'for blocking off explanation' (1969, 351). Contradictions are thus given ontological status, and, furthermore, their sources as myths are put back beyond memory and ordinary time (*ibid.*, 344). They are thereby removed from the mundane arenas of social dispute and conflict.[20] Finally, Leach shows that myth may function to *mask* contradictions and thereby make them tolerable (Leach, 1966; cf. Sperber, 1967).

Thus, both the charter and mediatory functions of myth sustain social configurations against such sources of malaise as strain, the passage of time, and the emergence of new and antagonistic forms and values.[21] But there is a third use of myth which would appear to accomplish the same objective, and this lies in its capacity to provide cognitive frameworks which construct social reality for the actor in particular ways. Maranda tells us that the study of myths reveals the ways in which alien structures are reduced to familiarity and, more generally, '. . . the culture-conditioning mechanisms that mould ethnic cognitive systems' (1972, 8). In this regard, myths would appear to serve as 'cognitive maps' (Bailey, 1971, 300, n. 2), exercising some control over what may be known and how what is known may be understood. A related competence of myth, which will be of particular relevance to the present study, is that as a cognitive map it may be used to mediate values and practices which are alien to a given cultural milieu in such a way that they appear to be entirely consistent with—and, perhaps, to have emerged from—the indigenous culture. Here again, then, the effect of the use of myth is to produce support for a particular set of social principles and relationships.

The charter, mediatory and cognitive functions of myth would thus seem to have in common an obvious relevance and similarity to the processes I associate with political legitimisation. They combine to present a picture of the uses and management of political myth which amount to the attempt to 'bridge the gap' between a 'sacred', rhetorical world of legitimated and unquestioned values and the mundane world of questionable behaviour and problematic experience. A value is drawn from a mythic system of order and attached to an empirical system of order; that, in analogical terms, is the essence of political legitimisation. When one actor seeks to legitimate his political relation to another there is an implicit or explicit reference to social doctrine which legislates the values of the relation. This doctrine may be continually elaborated and mediated through interaction. Following Malinowski (especially 1963*b*) I would suggest that myth be regarded as the 'concretisation' of these doctrinal principles. In its political applications myth may thus be seen as the means by which one assumes or portrays the consistency of structures with the principles of the social order as they are expressed in ideology or doctrine. Thus it both legitimates the structures, and achieves or maintains the valued order—the *raison d'être* of politics. Political legitimisation is accomplished through the management of myths by inducing others to accept the values you impute to particular social forms. The object of legitimisation is to persuade an 'audience' that the empirical political order replicates the mythic order from which the values which structure the political relation are derived.

THE MANAGEMENT OF MYTHS

Myth, then, is directed towards the affirmation and legitimisation of the principles which govern, or are said to govern, social relations and organisation. The myths with which I deal in this study are rarely manifest as coherent narratives. They are more often idealised conceptions of forms of social organisation and behaviour which are symbolically expressed in the leaders' strategic presentations of themselves. Such expressions often have about them the flavour of ritual, in the sense of formalised behaviour which has the effect of imposing some sort of normative order on social relations.[22] Often they are manifest as 'condensation symbols' with which ideologies and partisan philosophies are indigenously associated.[23] Essentially, though, the myths are models of the opposed constructions of reality which define the confrontation of leadership groups in Focaltown and which are underpinned by the emerging cultural and material dualisms which inform social life in the community.

The natures of these contrasting myths suggest their most appropriate forms of management. This book is concerned with two such modes, which I call 'cultural extension' and 'cultural substitution'.

All of the commentators on myth whom I mentioned above see myth referring to some prior point in a society's history, rooting the present in the past and, in so doing, legitimating the present by investing it with the values which have become sacralised by their very historical or traditional nature. The point is made succinctly by Worsley (1970a, 217):

Men ransack the past to find legitimations for the present: they discover precursors, trace intellectual pedigrees, re-write history.

It is this kind of myth management that I refer to as cultural extension. It is used to sustain the legitimacy of the customary leadership in Focaltown and is therefore designed to coincide with and (culturally) extend the prevalent belief system, adapting it to the structural exigencies of modern conditions.

But in Focaltown there is another kind of myth as well, which points not to a sacralised past, but to a social order which is in the cultural 'future'. Indeed, it declares the irrelevance of the past and the need to replace it by structures and values drawn from 'modern' societies elsewhere. It therefore proposes the substitution of indigenous values by culturally alien ones. It seeks to reject and replace the prevalent belief system, and to (culturally) substitute them by values which sustain an 'alien' set of structures. I suggest that the doctrine comprised of such values may be analogous to myth largely because of its processual similarity. But, further, there seems to be implied in many descriptions of myth a quality of timelessness which might point to an hypothetical future as well as to an unsubstantiated past.[24] It is the management of such 'future'-oriented myths in Focaltown that I call cultural substitution.

The management of myths to accomplish political legitimisation is the attempt to stabilise and solidify political relationships by mobilising supportive values. It is therefore frequently associated with instability.[25] Political myth expresses the value of a system of order, and thus becomes most salient when that system of order is called into question. If the myths are wanting in the performance of their functions, political change may occur, although their inadequacy constitutes neither a necessary nor a sufficient condition for change to take place. It does suggest, however, that the legitimacy of the political order has become problematic.

The particular political order with which this book deals is itself constituted by legitimacy. Legitimacy is the valued resource which structures the political relationships between the two antagonistic elites, and between the elites and the community in which each seeks its support. The competition for legitimacy was largely brought about by the challenge of an emergent elite to the established power and legitimacy of its rival, on the grounds that the social order from which the latter drew its legitimating—mythic—values had become historically irrelevant and, indeed, pernicious. It sought legitimacy for itself on the basis of values drawn from a putatively more appropriate 'modern' order. The situation is thus one which clearly illustrates the association between myth management and political instability or change. Myth management in Focaltown became critical when one system of order was challenged and therefore required to renew its legitimacy whilst, at the same time, the challenging system needed to establish its own. When the empirical relevance of the myths is called into question, the attempt is made to locate the values they express in empirical society. The concretisation of doctrine or 'abstract dogma' is taken a stage further than in Malinowski's formulation: it functions as an ideology not just in the normative sense, but in constructive or cognitive senses as well, providing particular frameworks for the interpretation of reality.

This, I would suggest is the distinctive feature of the *management* of myths. Thus cultural extension demonstrates the consistency of new or existing structures with traditional cultural values. But in so doing it implicitly asserts the prior and concrete existence of such values and structures: tradition is brought down from the level of vague historical possibility and grounded in 'actuality'. The myth here surely fulfills the function attributed to it by Malinowski, as 'a prototype for subsequent cases' (1963*b*, 309). Similarly, cultural substitution, whilst it rejects traditional values in favour of culturally new and, hence, alien ones, asserts not merely the desirability but implicitly also the *existence* of another, foreign order from which they are drawn.

These alternative strategies of myth management were given particular salience in Focaltown by the pace and extent of social change in the community and its hinterland. It was incumbent upon local leaders in Newfoundland at that time to express some philosophy of change, since the public life of the province was dominated by the various consequences of the government's development programme. Thus, the choice of myth-managing strategy among the Focaltown leaders was dictated by their modernising guises. A similar confrontation of strategies may be observed in many 'developing' societies. Cultural extension, for example, would describe Nyerere's defence of the single-party state in Tanzania, in which he argues essentially that parties are the political expression of opposing classes, and that since African society is traditionally classless, there is no need for more than one party (see, *inter alia*, Bienen, 1970; Glickman, 1965; 1967). In similar fashion, he justifies socialism—more exactly, 'African Socialism'—as the mere modernisation of traditional African communality (Nyerere, 1962). Similarly, in Newfoundland, Premier Smallwood defended the federal and provincial governments' controversial resettlement programme, under which whole communities ceased to exist, by arguing that people had been relocating in substantial numbers for years before there was a programme and that the governments' action was, therefore, no more than a rationalisation of customary practice (*Newfoundland Bulletin*, February 1970, 1). It is the kind of strategy to which Marriott gives the name of 'culture management' (1963, 35, 54), and which Hoselitz calls the use of 'tradition in development' (1961, especially 111). As an innovatory technique it is employed in modernisation not only by politicians but by planners as well, seeking to make their technologically 'rational' messages compatible with elements of what they regard as 'indigenous mentality' (Kavadias, 1966, 367; also Foster, 1962, 28).

The second strategy, cultural substitution, calls forth a rather more difficult and painful programme of management. It generally involves a fundamental change in the nature of political structures which are subsequently used to generate supportive values. Perhaps the most dramatic theoretical expression of cultural substitution is the Marxist–Leninist model of the proletarian dictatorship, whose structures are intended to produce a supportive 'consciousness'. It is further exemplified by Apter's concept of 'political religion', in which the state is given exceptional authority by being made the sole source of authority—both sacred and secular—and is accomplished by the politicisation of all social acts so that each may be seen as critical to the security of the state (Apter, 1963).[26] In practice it appears to be unlikely that such unfamiliar structures could be maintained over the long term without succumbing to some modification by the indigenous cultural context. It is even more unlikely that they could produce 'pure' supportive values: inevitably, they must be mediated by the cultural context on which they are imposed. They may change the prevailing culture, but they are also likely to be changed by it and by the modified cultural milieu. In this regard, it is now commonplace to locate the 'Marxism' of many socialist societies in their characteristic nationalisms as well as in nineteenth century German political thought. It is unrealistic to suppose that ideologies and their associated structures can simply be transported from one cultural milieu and imposed upon another without undergoing any change (cf. Hodgkin, 1964, 60). I do not propose here a reversion to the sterility of 'cultural drift' theory, because it appears to me incontrovertible that a culture can be substantially changed by deliberate means. The Chinese experience suggests that this is not necessarily a long drawn-out process. But I do suggest that alien structures and their ideologies, and indigenous cultural values mediate each other (cf. Kavadias, *op. cit.*, 370). Cultural substitution, therefore, is often to be found in persuasive rather than coercive strategies, and certainly in less extreme forms than those mentioned above. It is such a persuasive strategy that I discuss in the Focaltown context. Here the same element of structural imposition is present, but a deliberate attempt is made to 'sell' the new order, not only in terms of its intrinsic values, but also in terms of the value of change itself.[27]

It is in this respect that cultural substitution becomes particularly interesting as a strategy of legitimisation through myth management. For, like cultural extension, it is persuasive by nature. Its myths, as well as its proponents' structural and institutional manoeuvres, acquire importance. Indeed, we find in Focaltown that the efficacy of the culture-substitutors' attempts to legitimate themselves resides in their myth management rather than in the performances of their innovative institutions.

The contrasting presentational styles of the opposing leadership groups in Focaltown provide the clearest indication of the degree to which their legitimacy has become problematic. In the old days of oligarchic mercantile autocracy, the local elite had no cause for anxiety about its popular support: support was culturally enjoined, criticism regarded as culturally repugnant, and 'deference' was the typical attitude to authority. But in the contemporary context both the identity and the structure of leadership is in question. New and aspiring leaders have emerged; new organisations have fundamentally changed the institutional character of the community. The neo-ritualistic presentation of strategic public identities by the leaders through myth management is a means by which they attempt to impose at least the appearance of order and stability. These contrasting myth managing strategies of cultural extension and cultural substitution may be thought of as alternative approaches to the acquisition of legitimacy, the valued resource whose 'scarcity' structures the political relation between the two groups of leaders.

NOTES TO CHAPTER ONE

[1] All the local names used in this study are fictitious.

[2] These are the same considerations that underlie Evans-Pritchard's own discussion of politics in his study of the Nuer: 'By political values we mean the common feeling and acknowledgement of members of local communities that they are an exclusive group distinct from and opposed to other communities of the same order, and that

they ought to act together in certain circumstances and to observe certain conventions among themselves' (Evans-Pritchard, 1940, 264–5).

[3] See, for example, Wagner (1940, 201) for a succinct and explicit statement of this view.

[4] One may note here that the explanatory framework of 'function', whether based on an analogy with the organism (as in Durkheim's case) or with the cybernetic model (in Parsons') logically points to the postulation of 'normal'—or correct—functioning.

[5] He departs from Hobbes and Weber in his assertion that coercion and the use of force are not 'forms' of power, but are instruments which can be 'bought' with power. On these grounds he distinguishes 'value in exchange' (power) from 'value in use' (instruments). See Parsons (1969, 518).

[6] Homans makes a similar criticism of functionalism as such. It was, he says, '... more interested in the consequences than in the causes of an institution, particularly in the consequences for a social system considered as a whole. The consequences were the *functions* of the institution.' (Homans, 1971, 103).

[7] The irony of Parsons' approach is that by making the consensus *prior* to politics he makes politics non-political, for he partly explains the capacity to implement rules by the sanctions authority is permitted to apply to collectivity members if they default on their obligations. But the jurisdiction to apply sanctions, like the extent of obligation, is held in his model to be determined by 'legally' restricted power—the rules originating in the 'legality' rather than in the power which it produces and sanctions. And this legality does not stem from the political ('goal attainment') subsystem at all, but from the 'integrative' and 'pattern maintenance' subsystems. In other words, we may infer from his theory the suggestion that the capacity to implement rules, or to secure obeisance—that is, to exercise power effectively—is not 'political', but is enshrined in some analytically distinct set of processes. This position is made yet more perplexing by his insistence that the four subsystems are functionally discrete and autonomous.

[8] The circularity may be summarised as follows: (1) the function of the polity is to achieve collective goals; (2) action is legitimate when pursued for collectivity ends; (3) collectivity generates politics; (4) political action is collectivity-based; (5) collectivity-based action is legitimate; (6) therefore, politics is legitimate, because (7) it is action pursued for collectivity ends.

[9] It is further expressed in his conceptualisation of the political system as the means whereby 'inputs' are converted into 'outputs' (1957, 384).

[10] This attribution of political action to authoritative roles is congruent with Easton's stipulation of 'society' as the level at which politics is found: he is talking, of course, about government. The authoritative allocation is made—political action taken—when differences within society appear to be irreconcilable and threaten its stability (1965a, 53). Politics, then, becomes the application of a formula for 'settlement' to a conflict situation by a legitimated body—a conception more explicitly and flexibly stated by Miller (1962, 14 ff.). Thus, to talk of politics as the authorative *allocation* of values, rather than more generally as behaviour oriented towards the allocation of values—a generalisation to which Easton aspires but does not attain—is simply to dress up the earlier definitions of politics as 'governmental activity' in new clothes (cf. Bailey, 1968, 281).

But, further, it reflects his tendency (notwithstanding his use of the term 'interaction') to see politics as inhering in role rather than action. The tendency is reflected in his distinction between 'member' and 'analytic' systems, and in the correlation of allocative power with organisational hierarchy (even in parapolitical systems). He is continually led to distinguish one kind of interaction from another on the basis of the roles involved. That is tantamount to saying that he infers the nature of behaviour from the 'system' (political, economic, etc.) to which the role pertains: he derives behaviour from role. It would seem to me that the logic of the grounded theory/interactionist perspectives must demand that, analytically, the role should be inferred from the behaviour.

[11] Leach does suggest that his own model is not simply a piece of analytic fiction but '... corresponds to the way the Kachins themselves apprehend their own system through the medium of the verbal categories of their own language' (*op. cit*, ix).

[12] This is by no means to reiterate the structural functionalist precept that power is only power if it is legitimate. Rather, it is to suggest that power is only power if it is recognised as such—i.e. if it works—and legitimacy *may* help it to work a little better.

[13] It is the incorporation of such hidden variables into explanations of behaviour which makes the 'inside knowledge' type of journalism so intriguing. Such journalism is often stigmatised as sensational—but really, perhaps, because it gives the lie to public appearances or overt explanations. This is precisely the kind of otherwise inaccessible explanation which participant observation makes possible in academic sociology.

[14] I use strategy here in a general sense, to include all the manipulations, manoeuvring and management processes involved in an actor's attempt to organise social interaction.

[15] The literature on power is appallingly prolific and is sufficiently well known not to need specific citations here. It is marked by a profusion of attempts, frequently in connection with community power studies, to stipulate exclusive structural loci of power. Dissatisfaction with these procedures has been widely expressed, most notably, perhaps, by Bachrach and Baratz (1962) and March (1966). A recent attempt to avoid stipulating structural referents is White's notion of power as 'significant affecting' (1972, 489), although Danzger (1964) points out the difficulties of using the qualifications 'salient' or 'significant'.

[16] That is not to say that such behaviour can *only* be explained as if it were political. It suggests merely that it is behaviour which is intelligible in similar terms to those which we commonly or colloquially call 'political': people arrange themselves, or are arranged into systems of differentiation with respect to particular valued resources. It is better thought of as behaviour with *a political dimension*.

[17] A *commodity* only becomes a *resource* when it is valued, that is, when it is recognised to be a resource—to have some potency. Legitimisation is frequently the process by which this comes about in political behaviour. Put this way, I am turning Weber and Easton's (1965b,'287 ff.). theories of legitimacy on their heads. For they see legitimacy as *deriving* from the resources which sustain regimes in power. I am arguing that it is *to* the resource employed in interaction that legitimacy is primarily accorded (cf. Worsley, 1970b, 288; also D. L. Cohen, 1972, 300–1).

[18] I emphasise that I am suggesting only that the leaders' legitimating devices *resemble* mythic behaviour. Whether or not they may be properly categorised as *being* mythological is for the reader to decide.

[19] Cohen, appropriately enough in the Malinowski Memorial Lecture, also emphasises the function of myth's historical nature, arguing that it serves to 'anchor the present in the past' (1969, 349).

[20] One might add that contradictions may become sacralised in this way, being expressed in such institutionalised beliefs as that the political leader, like the soccer referee, 'knows best', that there is 'free speech' and 'equality of opportunity', and in such conventions as the 'white wedding' and professional/amateur distinctions in international sport.

[21] Though charter myths *justify*, as well as merely explain, a given system of social order; cf. Balandier (1970, 118).

[22] I do not wish to engage in debate on the meaning or functions of ritual, fraught, as it is, with anthropological controversy. It will be clear, however, that my use of the word is closer to the 'instrumentalist' traditions (Lienhardt, 1961; Douglas, 1966; Goffman, 1971; 1972) than to those which see ritual as merely expressive or symbolic acts (Radcliffe–Brown; Parsons), or as standardised and repetitive behaviour (Nadel, 1954; Goody, 1961). Further, I would suggest that there are aspects of the leadership confrontation in Focaltown which would seem to have a striking affinity with various characteristics which different writers have attributed to ritual. Gluckman's suggestion

(1962, 34) that ritual increases with the need to distinguish undifferentiated roles has an obvious relevance to the nature of the Focaltown political elite, as does Douglas' (1966, 62) that its incidence varies with the intensity of social interaction. Similarly, there are valuable insights into Focaltown politics to be gained from Turner's associations of ritual with crisis and insecurity (1969, 8, 10) and with the concealment of conflict (eg. 1967, 265), and his remarks on the political implications of ritual office (1967, especially 206, 263–4; also 1966).

[23] An interesting analysis of the uses to which such condensation symbols may be put is by Laponce (1969). A more general discussion of the uses of symbolism in political process is to be found in Edelman (1964).

[24] Percy Cohen (1969, 351) suggests that future-oriented 'myth-like' phenomena should more properly be called 'prophecy', but the distinction appears to be arbitrary. The processual nature and functions of the two kinds of myth are similar.

[25] Cf. Turner on ritual (*above*).

[26] The literature on social movements is, of course, full of instances of the politicisation of social action in explicit opposition to the state. See, for example, Worsley (1970*b*) and Willener (1970).

[27] Some writers see this as a characteristic feature of contemporary development process in which change is intentionally stimulated (cf. Costa Pinto, 1965, 466).

CHAPTER TWO

The setting

THE HISTORICAL BACKGROUND

The community reported here—Focaltown—represents in particularly dramatic form the extent and nature of the change which is engulfing Newfoundland. In certain respects it approximates the model of the 'modernised' community which has been implicit in the province's development policies since Confederation with Canada in 1949. In this regard its most important feature is its industrial economic base. There is hardly any fishing prosecuted from Focaltown. Instead the work force is engaged primarily in mining and logging and also in retail and service capacities. It was the explicit aim of Premier Joseph Smallwood, the man who led Newfoundland into Confederation and directed her government for the ensuing twenty-two years, that the fishery should be replaced as the mainstay of the outport economy by extractive and manufacturing industry. However, his early campaign promise of 'two jobs for every man' failed to materialise. Starved of stable industrial employment and with the fishery forced into dismal decline (see especially Brox, 1972), many men in rural Newfoundland have turned to 'welfare' as the only viable economic adaptation available to them (see Wadel, 1969; 1973).[1] Thus, whilst the image of thriving affluence that Focaltown presents to the world is not mere illusion, it certainly does not tell the whole story. The high incidence of unemployment is complemented also by fear of unemployment among those who do have jobs, and the constantly expressed pessimism about the viability of the local mines has created a feeling of insecurity which appears to be widespread among the population.

There is, then, a dualism in Focaltown's industrialised modernity which distinguishes the recipients of its material benefits from those who are deprived, or even fear to be deprived, of those benefits and from those who have been deprived of customary subsistence forms by the exigencies of economic change. It is a dualism which underpins, without wholly explaining, the dualism which defines the competing groups of activists among the community's leadership. These opposing alignments may be spoken of, in general terms, as representing the conflict between the customary and parochial values of traditional leadership and political articulation, and those of a culturally alien, self-consciously 'North American' style of political domination. They breed mythologies of, respectively, syncretism and innovative entrepreneurialism.

We return to the leadership conflict later. For the moment, the changes referred to must be put into perspective, for their fundamental and pervasive consequences are not adequately served by the description of mere transition from subsistence to industrial economy. It is the profusion of related changes, as they affect outport people in their everyday lives and thereby structure community life, to which I want to draw attention. My purpose is not well served either by a statistical digest, for it is not the *fact* of structural change but its implication for the diffuse values by which leaders legitimate themselves that I wish to emphasise.

The 'modernisation' of Newfoundland has been crammed into the relatively few years which have passed since Confederation with Canada in 1949. By 'modernisation' I mean here no more than Newfoundland's sudden deviation from her traditional, solidly entrenched, and hitherto virtually unchanging social organisation. For five hundred years the country had suffered the worst excesses of colonialism, and of physical and cultural isolation. As the creature of insatiable mercantile interests, its economy was exploited through the rape of resources and the imposition of vicious financial systems of credit and truck which combined with the ecological conditions to keep the great majority of the rural population at subsistence or sub-subsistence levels. The scattered and isolated outports were subservient to the merchants of St John's, the capital. By and large, the fishermen in the outports were subservient to the local merchants who outfitted them and took their fish in partial exchange. The fishermen thus stood at the very abyss of powerlessness, dependent upon the vicissitudes of the cod fishery, and on the whim of the local merchant. He had no voice in the outside world, nor any easy means of reaching it. He had no cash. He lived on the fish he landed, the meat he trapped or shot, the vegetables he managed to grow on Newfoundland's shallow soil, and berries he gathered in the fall of the year. If any of these failed there was no alternative source of subsistence. The methods of fish catching and curing barely changed over the centuries. As the dynamic economies of the North American mainland grew, so Newfoundland's stagnated, relieved only by the temporary prosperity gained from other people's wars. There was large-scale emigration, first to the 'Boston States' and later to Ontario.[2] It is against this impressionistic historical background, which persisted into the middle of this century, that one must set the consumer society that Newfoundland was becoming—and typified, in this regard, by Focaltown—at the time of this research. Modern schools, houses, roads, cars, television, town councils, development committees, service clubs, all the paraphernalia of 'mainland' social life, and all acquired over a very short space of time.

It is little wonder, then, that the traditional structures of leadership were propelled into crises of legitimacy. The merchant could no longer maintain his dominion by the fact of his virtual monopoly of the outporter's source of livelihood. He could no longer maintain his authority and prestige by representing the community to the outside world, and interpreting the world for his local clients. He was being overtaken by the availability of information from the mass media, by the competition from other aspiring leaders, by the relative ease of access to the outside world. Leadership in the traditional society was gained by ascriptive and exclusive criteria, or won by the rewards of the occupational skill of the fisherman. These customary bases ceased to be sacrosanct. Leadership was now becoming a matter for competition, and what constituted *legitimate* leadership became an issue for dispute between competing leaders. It is in such a situation of flux and instability that aspiring leaders articulate myths and rituals designed to secure their legitimacy—and, thereby, a degree of permanence and valued order.

An introduction to the description of these processes requires first some discussion of certain important aspects of this period of change which set the empirical context for the struggle for legitimisation between the Focaltown leaders.

Smallwood
First, then, I refer briefly to certain elements of the general situation of social change which have some relevance to the problem of legitimate leadership in Focaltown.

One of the features of public and governmental affairs in Newfoundland —and, more generally, in Canada—which forcibly strikes the British observer is the enormous salience of personalities in politics. Whilst one is wary of 'great men theories', it seems clear that the history of Newfoundland society since Confederation in 1949 cannot be adequately understood without some appreciation of the extraordinary and overwhelming influence of Joseph Smallwood, the man who spearheaded the prolonged struggle for Confederation and went on to become the first premier of the Province of Newfoundland, an office he held for twenty-two years. I have no intention of entering upon biographical or evaluative discussions of the man, for these have been offered in plenty (see especially Gwyn, 1968; Smallwood, 1973). What concerns me here is the impact of the Smallwood experience upon the values with which Newfoundlanders regard their leaders. Smallwood manipulatively employed his intimate knowledge of Newfoundland political culture to sustain him in all manner of campaigns. A compendium of such Smallwoodiana would be too large to undertake here, but there are a number of items which invariably appear both in popular accounts and in the discussions of journalists and academics. Exploiting customary values he won the battle for Confederation against the opposition of the St John's merchantocracy (Gwyn, *op. cit.*; Smallwood, *op. cit.*; Noel, 1971; Horwood, 1969; Perlin, 1968).

He flaunted his position as Patron Supreme. He personally selected all Liberal candidates for the provincial and federal legislatures. He contrived an image of himself as the entire government of Newfoundland, handling personally a settlement's request for a wharf or a public telephone, as well as the negotiations for massive loans in the international money market. Daily he interpreted the world's affairs to an avid Newfoundland radio audience, as he had done in the days before he entered politics. He continually engineered incredible and dubious financial arrangements with prospective investors which must have brought a man anywhere else into immediate and lasting disrepute. He did battle with successive federal governments, visited heads of government around the world, made men's careers and as easily destroyed them. Some examples of his involvement at all levels of Newfoundland's life will be found in the chapters which follow. Smallwood dominated Newfoundland. As a politician, he towered above his contemporaries. He made opposition to himself appear illegitimate. Year after year he harangued his listeners into adulation, submission, or stunned incredulity. In all this he utilised the conspicious values of the rural political culture and adapted the customary structures of traditional community life. Thus he exploited the outporters' reluctance to participate in decision-making, he reinforced their political reticence and dependency, he maintained the old institutions of brokerage, he capitalised on the cultural repugnance of criticism of existing leadership. Smallwoodism was neither ideology nor partisan doctrine: it was a movement of the low-income, traditionally deprived, and largely Protestant rural working class, which tied the mythic values of traditional social organisation to those of materialistic radicalism. It was a patronal populism in which Smallwood contrived to make himself appear as the only *legitimate* leader of Newfoundland, and then used his legitimacy as a valued and scarce resource to create and maintain his power.

This reads as an exaggerated and rather sensational account—but exaggeration is basic to the Idea of Smallwood. Its theoretical lesson for the general argument of this book is the notion of legitimacy as a political resource. For the moment, though, it will suffice to note that Smallwoodism is the style of leadership against which is set the competition for leadership in Focaltown. It defines and sustains the 'traditional' and syncretic elite, and epitomises the values and structures against which the entrepreneurial elite struggles, with its messages of modernity and rationalism.

The dominion of 'Joey' Smallwood is one dimension of the situation which characterised Newfoundland at the time this study was made.[3] Those others which I discuss briefly are all related to it.

Resettlement
In the late 1960s, rural Newfoundland was caught in a crisis of insecurity brought about by what was variously known as the resettlement, relocation

and centralisation programme, operated by the Provincial government's Department of Community and Social Development (see Matthews, 1970; Wadel, 1969; Iverson and Matthews, 1968; Skolnik, 1968). The purposes of this programme were to reduce the proliferation of small communities scattered around Newfoundland's coastline in order to enable a more efficient and economic distribution of services and to build population centres for planned industrialisation. The decline of the inshore fishery had deprived many of these communities of their traditional form of subsistence, and they were being forced to welfare or to other disruptive adaptations in order to survive at all (cf. Wadel, *op. cit.*). The correctness or otherwise of the resettlement policy is not my present concern. Rather, I limit myself simply to the suggestion that, because of the way the programme was managed and reported, talk and fear of resettlement appeared to play a critical part in the way that the surrounding settlements of Focaltown defined their problems. Matthews (1970) reports instances of how *information* about resettlement provided by the government was interpreted by communities as announcements of the government's *intention* to resettle them immediately. Thus, settlements which had not previously considered moving suddenly found themselves committed by the statutory petition to relocate. The carrot dangled by the government was the financial grant available to relocating families. A relatively large amount of cash offered to those habituated to near-subsistence living was surely attractive.

Resettlement was an unpopular idea in many outports, and not just because it frequently succeeded in creating only a greater concentration of people dependent on welfare. Communities continually sought protection against resettlement, largely by attempting to obtain amenities such as electricity, water, community stages, and so forth, which would preclude their subsequent relocation on the grounds of its obvious wastefulness. This kind of concern paid particular dividends to those local leaders who built their careers upon their acuity as brokers between the locality and the government, such as those we meet in one of the Focaltown leadership groups I discuss later. The more positive strategy of seeking to make the threatened community economically viable was rarely propagated, for reasons which, again, I discuss later. One of these I mention here, though, for it serves also to relate the general issue of resettlement to the politics of leadership in Newfoundland. The interests of both of the competing groups of leaders in Focaltown—and, for that matter, of the major opposed groups at the provincial level—made it impolitic to encourage independence among local settlements, for both groups sought 'captive' constituencies: the traditionalistic group required a dependent population; the entrepreneurial elite sought a passive and submissive public. The logic of their respective stances was to maintain their statuses as leaders, that is, to maintain the public's 'need' for the leadership they would provide—to maintain the division and distance between leaders and led.

The struggle in which they were engaged was for legitimacy as a resource of leadership; it was, essentially, a struggle *between leaders*. It was most certainly not a struggle whose object was to redistribute the resources of leadership among the population as a whole. Leaders were to remain leaders; followers were to be led.

Resettlement, then, was a symptom of the powerlessness of the outport working class, and can be understood as more than an aspect of Smallwood's development policies: it is also a product of the essential nature of leadership in rural Newfoundland, which has been sustained and reinforced in the Smallwood years. Resettlement, then, is a significant background issue to our discussions in that, firstly, it created an insecurity among Focaltown's hinterland settlements on which both of the competing elites tried to capitalise; and secondly, it indicates the nature of the Focaltown struggle as being one between leaders in which the institution of elite or socially distant leadership is not in question.

Competing leadership
Both of these characteristics also informed the other great issue of public discussion during the period of my research, which concerned the leadership of the provincial Liberal Party and, thereby, also the premiership. Until 1968 Smallwood's position was unquestioned. At election after election he swept back to power leaving the opposition Progressive Conservative Party generally with just the mere handful of seats they managed to collect, mostly in St John's. Whilst Smallwood reigned unchallenged, the Progressive Conservatives went through leader after leader. The essential stability of Smallwood's administration was broken only by the very occasional resignations from his Cabinet. His government survived successive crises and scandals with little apparent loss of public support. The tide began to turn, however, in 1968 when, following Pierre Trudeau's election as leader of the federal Liberal Party, the Newfoundland Liberals lost all but one of their federal seats. Smallwood's monolithic control of the Newfoundland electorate had previously made the province a secure base for the federal party, and it was therefore astonishing that the seats should have been lost against the considerable national 'swing' to the Liberals. Smallwood's explanation claimed that the result was produced by some literature imported into Newfoundland depicting Trudeau as the Antichrist. Whatever the reasons, Newfoundlanders suddenly realised that Smallwood *was* vulnerable.

Immediately prior to the election Smallwood had been overtaken by another crisis. He had for some time been negotiating with an American financier, upon whose reputation some doubt had been locally cast, for the construction of an oil refinery. Two of his most prominent younger ministers, John Crosbie and Clyde Wells, resigned, ostensibly over the terms of the refinery contract. Smallwood had previously suggested that he would resign the premiership during the following year to make way for 'a younger man'. The suggestion was not taken very seriously since he had made it on several previous occasions, but Crosbie decided to declare his candidacy for the Leadership, hoping, perhaps, that his active campaign might at least force Smallwood to declare his real intentions. Finally, Smallwood announced that he would resign, but would contest the leadership again.

The Crosbies were traditionally one of the most powerful of the St John's merchant families—the 'merchant princes' whom Smallwood had loved to castigate in his earlier oratory. The contest between the premier and John Crosbie was therefore conducted with great bitterness and all of the considerable deviousness which had traditionally characterised Newfoundland's governmental affairs. It raged for a year, and coincided with the development of local Liberal Associations based on mass membership. In fact, members were recruited into the Party by the two campaign teams in order to elect their respective slates of delegates to the leadership convention. Late in the campaign a third candidate—Alex Hickman—entered the hustings. He, also, was a minister in Smallwood's government, and had been widely regarded as one of Smallwood's most likely successors. In the event Smallwood won the leadership on the first ballot, and subsequently both Crosbie (after an interim during which he led his own party) and Hickman joined the Progressive Conservatives.

The result is not particularly significant for our purposes. The more important point is that real contestation among leaders had been restored to Newfoundland after an interval of many years.[4] Communities had been split or disturbed by the contest. The idea of the possibility of opposed groups of leaders had become recognised. Perhaps most important of all, traditionally legitimate leaders now found it necessary to engage with entrepreneurial or 'meritocratic' opponents in a struggle for legitimacy and the ascendancy from which they could define new and appropriate values of legitimate leadership. It is in the context of this kind of confrontation, and the change in political values which it bespoke, that the contest between the opposed groups of leaders in Focaltown must be set.

Class
The rise of the new leadership aspirants, marked by the organised opposition to Smallwood of entrepreneurs and professionals, signifies the emergence in the outports of a rural bourgeoisie. Social stratification in the Newfoundland outport was, traditionally, a simple form of organisation. At the top was the merchant, accompanied in those communities where they were resident by the priest and the magistrate. Beneath was the rest of the population—fishermen, tied by credit obligations into a neo-feudal relationship with the merchant. Of course, status differentials existed among the fishermen, but seem to have been associated more with occupational skills than with the ownership of property. Egalitarianism between owners and non-owners in fishing communities, as between

skipper and crew, remains important (see Faris, 1972; Nemec, 1972b; Stiles, 1972). Confederation in 1949, and the subsequent translation of the economy from credit and subsistence to cash bases has gradually altered this simple structure. In the larger communities, such as Focaltown, the monopolistic merchant house has given way to a class of businessmen competing in the provision of wholesale and retail services. Fish are now bought by regional processors. And where, previously, income differences would have been obscured by the homogeneity of consumption patterns within a community, there is now a tendency for consumption to become conspicuous, and differential status to be inferred accordingly. The pressure to consume is thus generated both by the external media, and by the 'internal' social forces of community life. As a result one of the most ubiquitous features of Newfoundland's communities is the credit and loan company offices. On all of this the merchants and shopkeepers thrive. In Focaltown they have acquired sufficient capital from the consumer boom of the 1960s to diversify their businesses to a surprising extent. In consequence there has emerged in the communities a consciousness of common interest among some businessmen—particularly among those whose commercial careers are directly attributable to the changes which followed from Confederation—which has had its effect on the wider structure of community life. In class and income terms the community is losing its social and physical integration. The assumption of a community identity, always problematic in this area of Newfoundland, was now further deterred by incipient class identity. Middle-class organisations such as Chambers of Commerce, Masonic Lodges, and Lions Clubs have proliferated as the social life-styles of the different class-income sectors diverged.

These developments should not be thought of in such exaggerated terms as class polarisation, for they were, rather, *incipient* phenomena. Nevertheless they were, perhaps, further established in Focaltown than in other Newfoundland communities of similar size, and they, again, define the context of the confrontation of leadership which is discussed later. It is clear that as a community changes in structure with an increasing diversification of interest along sectional lines, so the nature of its leadership, and of the conception of what constitutes *legitimate* leadership, will also change. Thus, whilst the two groups of leaders are, themselves, middle-class in the rather diffuse sense that class has in the outport milieu, we find that their appeals differ, and are made to essentially distinct sectional constituencies: the 'traditional' syncretic group looks to the outport proletariat and low-income population; the entrepreneurs appeal to their middle-class peers and to upwardly-mobile groups in the community.

The outport working class has traditionally been politically quiescent and submissive. Its only political movement of any importance prior to Confederation was the Fishermen's Protective Union, which flourished briefly in the years immediately before and during the First World War (see Feltham, 1959; Smallwood, 1927). The Union later foundered on the temptations of commerce and mercantilism; and soured, perhaps, by this experience, radical working-class politics, in the form of trades union or co-operative activity, has been almost entirely absent from Newfoundland. In some respects, the movement led by Smallwood for Confederation showed aspects of class-based aspirations, although the campaign was fought along many dimensions, not least being the religious. Smallwood himself, though in his younger days a socialist activist in New York and a union organiser in Newfoundland in the 1920s, earned a reputation for antipathy to labour activity. During his long reign he broke a particularly bitter woods workers' strike and subsequently outlawed the union involved, and made disruptive activity illegal for various groups of workers. As I suggested in the context of the resettlement issue, his longevity was based largely on his ability to maintain the outports in a state of dependency by reinforcing their disinclination to organise for collective action. The entrepreneurial elites have no interest in seeing any greater participation by the grass-roots, for their style of leadership depends upon the unfettered domination of community affairs by the businessmen's organisations. In this respect, we again encounter the limitation of the leadership struggle in Focaltown to the level of leadership itself.

In 1970 there appeared the first manifestation of working-class organisation since the demise of the Fishermen's Protective Union, in the guise of a new fishermen's union founded on the north-west coast. During the months that followed, its membership grew with some rapidity, and the union began to confront the fishplant owners, with varying degrees of success. At about the same time, two or three experimental producers' co-operatives were recognised to be operating with some success, and the various districts of the Province began to spawn regional development associations. All of this represented a quite new departure in participatory politics for Newfoundland, where participation had previously been negligible. The new militancy did not strike Focaltown, and that it did not is perhaps an indication of the success with which the competing elites protected the institution of exclusively-based leadership. When, therefore, I refer in the discussion which follows to the 'middle-class politics' or the 'rural proletariat' of Focaltown, I do not suggest a politics of class antagonism, but rather a contest of leadership styles and constituencies based upon the emerging recognition of diverging class interests.

Legitimate forms of community leadership
The conditioned reluctance of the outporters to participate in public affairs obviously makes suspect the motives of willing participants, and this renders particularly acute the crisis of legitimacy in which the community leaders find themselves. The most common assumption, not surprising in view of the history of government in Newfoundland, is that

politicians are self-seeking. It is a judgement which tends to be applied to local leaders as well, but is really the penalty paid for assertiveness. Leaders whose roles are based on traditional ascriptive criteria tend to escape suspicion, for they are perceived to lead because of those bases rather than because of any dubious motives. I refer later, also, to a quirk of Newfoundland political culture which attributes legitimacy to *incumbents* of leadership offices and denies it to their critics or aspiring replacements, and, further, to one which attributes legitimacy to structures or actors by virtue of their association with legitimated leaders. All of these phenomena lend legitimacy to the traditional elite in Focaltown and deny it to its entrepreneurial rivals. This argument is, of course, amplified in the case material which follows, but for the moment it throws into relief the general values with which community organisations are regarded.

Traditionally, community leadership was based simply on incumbency of an exclusive role—merchant, priest, and so on. Today, the outports have acquired more complex institutions. Focaltown overflows with organisations—the town council, Chamber of Commerce, Lions Club, school boards, Development Association and a host of others. But they are not alike as recipients of legitimacy. The town council is legitimate, largely because the 'traditional' (legitimated) leadership was associated with it. The Lions Club, which plays a much more active role in the initiation and formulation of policy, is not legitimated, for it is correctly perceived as the instrument of the entrepreneurs' activity and, therefore, as being symptomatic of assertiveness and implied criticism of the existing leadership. The suspicion of self-seeking denies legitimacy to the explicitly sectional organisations such as the Chamber of Commerce. There is, then, the paradox that organisation, generally, is culturally repugnant, whilst the town council is a legitimate organisation. This partly has to do with the essentially administrative nature of local councils in Newfoundland, but is intimately bound up with the phenomena I have been discussing. They serve, also, to show how the changing fabric of community life, now largely manifest in the proliferation of such institutions, constantly poses problems of legitimacy which underpin the competition in which the community leaders are engaged.

Welfare
The final element of the empirical situation to which I would draw attention here is the importance in the outport economy of welfare payments (see especially Brox, 1972; Wadel, 1969; 1973). There are various categories of welfare awards, from unemployment relief and sickness benefit, to child allowances and Unemployment Insurance Benefit. This abundance of financial aid is a direct consequence of Newfoundland's entry into Confederation and, for various reasons, has had an enormous impact on outport life.

In everyday speech in Newfoundland, being 'on welfare' is generally taken to refer to receipt of the dole. This is, itself, an indication of the high unemployment rate, as a consequence of which welfare becomes crucial as a source of income in outport economies. In many outports there is simply no regular or stable employment to be had, so that men who are not fishing or logging, and choose not to travel to the much sought-after construction jobs in other parts of the province, have to fill in with such part-time or occasional work as they can get. In this respect, whole communities become dependent upon welfare, and look to patrons and brokers for the provision of temporary employment. Thus the settlement, whether or not it has active fishermen, petitions for its community stage or wharf for the jobs its construction will provide.

A second explanation of the salience of welfare in the outports is that, with the exception of the dole, which is paid largely in vouchers, it is a source of *cash* income, particularly significant in a society for long constrained by the credit and subsistence bases of its economy. Cash allows people to compete for status in materialistic terms, and thus offers a wholly new identity to those available in the past. Furthermore, the monthly family allowance, paid for each child, is an important income for the typically large families of Focaltown and its hinterland.[5] The matter can be put simply. The transition of the economy to a cash basis has made the outport family dependent upon a cash income which, because of the paucity of jobs, has to be acquired from welfare sources. Even if a man has work he is subject to an unfamiliar pressure for cash. The cost of living is higher in Newfoundland than in mainland Canada, yet wages tend to be lower. In a community such as Focaltown it is becoming less common for men to build their own houses, and mortgage repayments—a charge which had never previously entered the outport family's household budget—pose an additional strain. All of these things are exacerbated by the novelty of cash and the sudden availability of 'luxury' consumer goods, and by the constant pressure to compete for status in the emergent materialistic milieu. The consumer society, during the period of this study, was not yet long enough established in rural Newfoundland for consumption levels and ceilings to be popularly recognised for different income groups. There was, therefore, no relief from the pressure to keep buying. Gargantuan television sets, washing machines, electric cookers, and freezers were common items in Focaltown households, whatever their income bracket.

This powerful materialistic ethos posed acute problems of identity for the fairly substantial sector of the population which simply could not engage in this status competition—that is to say, the sector *totally* dependent on welfare (see Cohen, 1975a). Although unemployment is so widespread it still carries a stigma.[6] There is a tendency in Focaltown to the development of something like a 'welfare class', which has been given greater coherence there by its concentrated membership of the Pentecostalist Assembly. We return here to the phenomenon of dualism with which this discussion of social change in Focaltown began. I suggest, again, that the dualism largely defines the nature of the confrontation of leadership groups in Focaltown for incorporated in the contending mythologies of legitimation are, on the one hand, an evocation of the traditional values of Newfoundland social life, directed largely towards this 'welfare class'; on the other, the strident messages of achievement and innovation whose intrinsic values are held to lie in their departure from those of the past.

FOCALTOWN

Despite the pace and intensity of change which struck the established organisation and values of social life in rural Newfoundland, styles of leadership and government were essentially conservative. Yet the rhetoric of leadership *was* couched in terms of change, and for many years it successfully obscured its exploitation of the traditional values and media of government in rural Newfoundland—patronage. Indeed, the cultural substitution of the entrepreneurial leaders emerged as the patronage system declined in salience and practicability, when Focaltown was sated with the typical dispensations of the patron, lacking only those which were now too expensive to provide. At this point, the demand for services, rather than the client-like supplication for favours, became a real political possibility. The period described in this study was marked by such change in the nature of relations in rural Newfoundland between the leaders and the led. The structures and values of patronage politics were still in evidence, but were entering upon their dotage. New institutions were springing up—political party organisations built upon local associations, service and fraternal clubs, economic development associations, and so on.

Focaltown epitomised this change and confrontation of political styles. It had not yet been affected by the radical activism of the producers' co-operatives and fishermen's locals which were appearing in other parts of the Province. Both of the competing groups of activists, though oriented to different class constituencies, were elitist by nature; each husbanded its exclusive resources of leadership and protected them from devolution even among its close and active supporters. The exclusivity of leadership to the middle class in Focaltown was not affected by the fundamental economic and infrastructural changes which had transformed the community over the previous two decades. The change had wrought a division among middle-class activists, but had not diminished their control over community affairs.

The roots of this division are thus to be sought less in a widespread demand for alternative leadership than in the development of the community itself and in the careers of its leaders. The latter comprise a long story, and are reserved to a separate chapter. For the moment, I will complete this discussion of the 'setting' with a brief description of Focaltown as the arena for the political struggle for legitimation.

Focaltown is the economic and service centre (cf. Wadel, 1969, 8) of Herring Bay on a coast of Newfoundland, and caters to a hinterland population of about 15,000. The bay is economically heterogeneous, with mining, logging, fishing, and some farming activity. The population is almost wholly Protestant, although divided among a variety of different denominations and sects. There is a small Catholic settlement, though Catholics account for only a tiny fraction of the population as a whole. First settled in 1870, the community of Focaltown was based on saw-milling, and timber has remained an important economic resource. For instance, two local businessmen own the only two independent logging companies in the province, each employing about 150 men. Around the turn of the century, a shipbuilding enterprise was started and, with diversification of local industry, attracting different skills, the community came to be solidly founded.

In 1909 the Anglo-Newfoundland Development Company began wood cutting operations for its paper mill at Nearby Town, and immediately before and during the First World War local timber was cut extensively and exported to Britain for use as pitprops. Apart from the logging companies mentioned above, the town boasts two construction companies operating on a Province-wide basis, two transportation companies, industrial supply, explosives, wholesale, and saw-milling businesses, as well as a full and competitive range of retail outlets. Perhaps most important is that the town served as a service, employment and housing base for the three copper mining companies which operated in the locality. The situation of the town and its commercial ascendancy made it a natural choice for the location of governmental and educational services, and Focaltown now has a fifty-bed hospital, a large regional high school, a separate denominational high school, a regional vocational training college, the regional library, magistrate's court, Welfare office, Royal Canadian Mounted Police headquarters, Fishery and Forestry Inspection offices, and Department of Highways depot, all serving the entire bay. The community is connected by eight miles of paved road to the Trans-Canada Highway, and has gravel all-weather road links to all of the surrounding mainland communities.

Thus, Focaltown's strategic position at the centre of Herring Bay, the influx into the area of industry, and the presence in the town of ambitious entrepreneurs, have made it one of the most rapidly growing communities in Newfoundland. Between 1940 and 1961, the population increased by 66 per cent, and between 1961 and 1969 by a further 75 per cent, to bring it to an estimated level in 1970 of 3,500.

Focaltown is almost exclusively Protestant, and has churches and their attendant organisations serving the Pentecostal, United Church, Salvation Army, and Anglican congregations. Typically, in Newfoundland, Pentecostal congregations grew with the declining evangelicalism of the United

Church (cf. DeWitt, 1969, 38), and in Focaltown it became the largest single denomination[7] and maintained a separate school system. However, religious denomination tends to be correlated with socio-economic status. Generally, Pentecostalism in Focaltown was associated with the lower end of the socio-economic scale. Salvationists tended to occupy a slightly higher category, and Anglicanism and Methodism were most concentrated in the upper reaches of the scale (cf. Crysdale, 1965, 2, 4–5). Of the seven activists with whom this book mostly deals, six belong to these high-status churches, all but one of them to the United Church. The religious homogeneity of some of the secular organisations in the town is reinforced by the Pentecostalists' proscription of the Lions Club—the most important voluntary association—and their general abstinence from commercial or entrepeneurial activity[8] which is reflected in their very low representation in the Chamber of Commerce. Whilst they profess an interest in politics and, as we shall see, are easily mobilised, the only civic organisation in which they have sought participation is the town council.

In addition to the churches there are some thirty administrative, political, social and service organisations. The town was incorporated in 1945[9] making it one of the earliest municipalities in Newfoundland. The Lions Club was founded in 1953, and grew to the point at which, collecting $15,000 annually (1968–70), it was the most successful and influential organisation in the community. Membership in the club is imperative for aspiring participants in the entrepreneurial politics of cultural-substitution. The club is used as a testing ground for these initiates and as an institutional façade by the culture-substituting elite. Perhaps its character can be best conveyed by comparing its relationship to Focaltown with that of the Booster's Club to Babitt's Zenith. The Chamber of Commerce was founded in 1966, and, up to the termination of my fieldwork, had stayed firmly in the control of the entrepreneurial activitists. Its membership paralleled that of the Lions Club, and the extent to which the organisations were interrelated was aptly expressed by a bemused bank manager who had just come to the community:

At the —— curling club, you could hold a meeting of the Focaltown Chamber of Commerce—as you could at any meeting of the Lions Club.

Both of these organisations were the creations of the entrepreneurial elite, as was the Economic Development Association, established in 1969. Whilst the activists of the competing group are members of all three, their mythic political style—as will become evident—denies the salience of organisational control.

The town also has Masonic and Orange lodges, a Junior Chamber of Commerce, a Canadian Legion branch, school boards, a Library Board, Volunteer Fire Brigade, political party district associations, Recreation Commission and sports associations, a Red Cross committee, a regular fortnightly newspaper, and a host of *ad hoc* committees.

The proliferation of organisations, however, does not reflect the typical individual's attitude to organisational involvement. Participation in most of these organisations is confined to a select group. A random sample of eighteen males showed that whereas seven belonged to an organisation, one man belonged to eight, and another to five organisations, while the rest belonged to only one or two. Further, only the first two belonged to organisations whose decisions might be said to have an 'important' effect on the community as a whole—the town council, Lions Club, Chamber of Commerce, Amalgamated School Board, and Economic Development Association. Of the thirty members of the Chamber of Commerce, twenty-four were Lions; of the seven members of the previous town council, five were Lions and four of these also belonged to the Chamber of Commerce. In the subsequent Council, four councillors belonged to both Lions and the Chamber. All of the Focaltown representatives on the Herring Bay Consolidated School Board were members of the Lions Club.

However, a simple statement of the overlapping membership of Lions and the other organisations and groups does not adequately demonstrate the source of power or the nature of political activity among the town's leaders. The Lions Club and, hence, the Chamber, contained within its membership the fundamental conflict of myth managing styles in which the competing elite structures become manifest. The conflict remained constant through all campaigns and issues which had the community as their primary object and was, indeed, reinforced by the intensive organisational activity of the town. For one effect of this activity was the institutionalisation, and consequent emphasis, of the distinct patterns of political behaviour and their associated myths.

There were, as I have mentioned, two such distinct patterns or strategies of myth management, each represented by a group alignment. The two strategies have been characterised as culture-extending and culture-substituting, and their groups will be called, respectively, the People's Group and the Sophisticates. The People's Group is composed of old-established residents who are closely associated with the traditional community leadership of the pre-expansion days in the late '50s and '60s, and who are at least second-generation Focaltowners. The Sophisticates are businessmen and professionals who have moved into the town within the last fifteen or twenty years and have, through their organisational initiative and incumbency of executive positions in organisations they have largely created themselves, challenged the traditional leadership of the community.[10] I discuss the composition of the groups and the characteristics of their members in the following chapter.

NOTES TO CHAPTER TWO

[1]Surveys made during the period of my fieldwork show that male unemployment in Focaltown varied between 19 per cent and 23 per cent. It is a volatile figure, as

there is a substantial degree of casual and part-year employment. These figures also include men classed by the welfare authorities as 'able-bodied' but who regard themselves as medically unfit for work.

[2]Emigration to mainland Canada continued through the period of my research. It has been estimated that between 1860 and 1966 there has been a net out-migration of 100,000 people (C. Herrick, personal communication, 1969). The population of Newfoundland in 1971 was 507,000.

[3]In fact the first major dent in Smallwood's supremacy occurred immediately prior to the commencement of this study, with the defeat of all but one of the Liberal candidates for Newfoundland ridings in the federal general election of June 1968. Thereafter the Province was plunged into an unprecedented contestation of leadership which was finally resolved by the victory of the Progressive Conservative Party at the Provincial general election of March 1972. Between these two dates both major parties had changed leaders and there had been an indecisive general election.

[4]The 'normal' processes of national leadership had been interrupted in 1933 by the decision to suspend the Dominion government and replace it with a Commision of Government appointed by, and responsible to, the British Colonial Office. There were six commissioners, three from Britain and three from Newfoundland. The legislature was abolished and with it what was, ironically, known as 'Representative' or 'Responsible Government' came to an end. The Commission of Government was essentially an interregnum in the highly volatile tradition of Newfoundland government. It ended when, following two referenda, Newfoundland renounced her Dominion status in order to enter the Canadian Confederation in 1949. The only major confrontation of leaders between the introduction of Commission Government in 1934, and the Liberal leadership campaign in 1969, was the opposed campaigns for Confederation and for the restoration of Responsible government. The issues and dimensions of this struggle were so complex that they went beyond the bounds of the mere contestation of leadership. For an interesting though partial account of Commission government see Lodge, 1939.

[5]Whilst family size, like income, tends to be correlated with religious denomination—Pentecostalists have the greatest number of children, Methodists have the fewest—families of eight or more children are not uncommon in the Focaltown area.

[6]For a highly sensitive ethnographic account of the stigmatic effects of being on welfare in this area of Newfoundland, and of the efforts made by an unemployed man to overcome them see Wadel (1973).

[7]The 1961 census shows the Pentecostal Assembly as the second largest denomination in Focaltown. With six adherents fewer than the United Church, it had 33.43 per cent of the population. However, the population of Focaltown has increased by approximately 75 per cent since then, and a survey I made in 1969 suggested that the Pentecostal Assembly accounted, at the time of the fieldwork, for some 42 per cent of Focaltown's inhabitants, an estimate confirmed by both of the local school boards. Much of this increase will have derived from in-migration, but some of it came from the Salvation Army.

[8]After I left Focaltown, a drug store run and patronised almost exclusively by Pentecostalists opened, in competition with one owned by an active associate of the 'culture-substituting' group. It was clearly more an expression of the leadership conflict than of some new-found commercial aspiration on the part of its Pentecostal manager, for it was financed almost entirely by members of the rival 'culture-extending' group.

[9]In 1945 two communities were incorporated into the one municipality. However, in 1961, Focaltown's growth—and pride—was such that the town elected to drop the other community (which had never enjoyed high repute), which subsequently became a Local Improvement District and, in 1969, was incorporated.

[10]There is also a third group, 'the Legitimisers', whose members and institutional settings are employed by both People's Group and Sophisticate activists in the search for legitimacy. I discuss them, in passing, later.

CHAPTER THREE

The myth managers

Both of the competing elites in Focaltown manage myths in the attempt to attribute value to the changed nature of social organisation and, thereby, to their own positions within it. As I suggested earlier, the myths are frequently expressed in aspects of the groups' behaviour which might helpfully be thought of as ritualistic. The myths are expressed in intra-group, as well as in inter-group interaction, and this is particularly the case in their articulation of their respective qualifications for leadership status.

I should briefly clarify my use of the terms 'group' and 'leader'. In neither case am I suggesting formal or contractual relationships. The members are characterised as *group* members by virtue of their observed common political styles, strategies and objectives. Whilst they are aware to some degree of their shared characteristics, they think of their opponents but not of themselves, as deliberately constituted groups (cf. Jacob and Teune, 1964, 4). The term 'leader' is applied to the member of the group who is observed to exercise the most influence on his fellow members and is most frequently their principal catalyst to action.

The groups' contrasting styles of myth management may be seen as informed by exclusive and distinguishing ethics which, with caution, might be thought of as those of ascription and achievement. Not surprisingly, the first would be associated with the syncretistic and 'traditional' myth managers—the People's Group—and the second with the entrepreneurial Sophisticates. I suggest the note of caution for the reason that, in terms of the mythic logic of requirements for office, any characteristic *qua* qualification has ascriptive dimensions: the values of achieved characteristics are *ascribed* rather than intrinsic and, furthermore, access to them is usually gained by other than strictly 'achieved' means.[1] However, because they are held and expressed by the groups as legitimations, I would suggest that their use as dichotomous types is empirically warranted.

The ascriptive characteristics stressed by the People's Group are those of its members' association with the traditional leadership of the community and with Smallwoodism, and their possession of well-founded family roots in the community. They emphasise their inclination towards or attempt to reconcile their behaviour with, the values of the traditional political culture. The Sophisticates, as achievers, lay great stress on their personal career successes, on their organisational innovations and skills, on the manifest superiority of the 'successful man', and, generally, on their dexterity in taking over the commercial and organisational leadership of the community from the traditional leaders. They seek to replace traditional values with those more appropriate to their mythically 'modern' order. As I menioned above, the values of these characteristics are expressed within the groups as well as between them, and indeed, these characteristics form valued resources which structure political relationships *within* the groups. (Thus, one is more or less intimately associated with Smallwood; one is more or less financially successful.) There is some competition for leadership, or for *apparent* leadership, within each faction, and it is this element which led me earlier to suggest that a 'minimalist' connotation be attached to my use of the word 'group'. Cohesiveness is often strained, particularly among the Sophisticates,[2] but the strain is always concealed from public view. This competitive element should not be exaggerated: the group members recognise their allies, acknowledge them, and make full use of their alliances. But in order that these internal differences should not be concealed and, indeed, that their similarities become evident, I discuss each of the seven major activists individually and in some detail. Hopefully, this discussion will illustrate the logic of the association between each of the groups and their members, and the strategies of myth management which I impute to them.

THE PEOPLE'S GROUP

The ways in which People's Group activists define their own histories reveals the fundamentally syncretistic nature of their culture-extending myth management. They seek to reconcile the present with the past—ideologies of change which respect and evoke the past—by showing that the new is either not really new at all but has its essential roots in the past, or by arguing that the 'new' socio-economic structures will be enhanced by traditional values which they preserve rather than deny. But, moreover, the activists themselves *personify* the syncretism. They have associations with and attributes of the traditional leadership, but play their roles in ways which would traditionally have been anathema. They have been forced into new commercial and political guises by the exigencies of political competition and social change: they fight elections, where before none would have been necessary; they engage in competitive cash enterprises—supermarkets and bars—where previously they would have operated as the monopolistic source of credit. They join the largely Sophisticate organisations—although they do not participate actively within them—in order not to appear isolated from the hustle and bustle of community affairs. Their myth-managing strategy of cultural-extension has, therefore, not merely to reconcile the present with the past but, also, their real personal situations with the traditional ascriptive images to which they aspire and for which they strive.

In consequence, these three myth managers all assume slightly different personae. The first, Arthur Martin who, as the eldest son, is the activist most intimately associated with the traditional leader, adopts his father's typically paternalistic stance. The second, Thomas Rodgers, 'the ordinary man's ordinary man', who, as an employee of Martin's father, became the town's first mayor, is the nearest Focaltown has to a populist—and this particular aspect of his affinity to Premier Smallwood is no accident. The third activist, Stan Lester, resorts—somewhat clumsily—to the career of political broker. In this respect, he plays a role typical of outport men ambitious for political careers in the service of Joe Smallwood. But, to a perhaps untypical extent, he fails to appreciate the degree to which Smallwood actually controls his role. I discuss each of these men in turn.

From the 1920s until 1954, the commercial and governmental affairs of Focaltown rested almost entirely in the hands of the Martin family. Their commercial enterprise in Focaltown began with their operation of a general store and with their direct participation in the herring fishery, and was run by Mrs Martin and two of her sons, Jacob and Edward. As the community's merchant, they held the traditional position of monopolistic dominance in the town, dealing strictly in credit (cf. Newfoundland Royal Commission, 1933, 79–80 (paras. 213–14)). When, later, their logging business had been established, credit was extended to their woods workers, in lieu of cash, redeemable at their store. The retail business really changed to cash transaction only when they began to pay the woods workers in cash. An early dispute between the Martins and the man who was later to move to Focaltown and become the Sophisticates' leader concerned the latter's intention to pay *his* men in cash, thereby setting a precedent harmful to the Martins' business practices.

In the early 1930s the Martins developed an independent pulpwood operation, and during the Depression cut lumber which they shipped to Wales to be used for pitprops. This business formed the foundation of the family's not inconsiderable fortune. During the Second World War they contracted with the Anglo-Newfoundland Development Company to cut lumber and operate the Company's saw-mills, located in Focaltown, and to ship the lumber, used for dunnage, in their own schooner to Closeport from where it would be exported to Britain. After the war they resumed pulpwood cutting for Bowaters and since then have cut an average of 30,000 cords per year, their woods operation employing up to 130 men and being one of only two large-scale independent logging companies in the province. (The other is owned by the leader of the Sophisticates.) Throughout this time they also had a transport business serving passengers, freight, and the mails, and, of course, the retail business was developing. In 1952 Mrs Martin died, leaving the business in the hands of her two sons and Edward's son Arthur. In 1964 Arthur's brother James joined the business and they opened a modern supermarket, followed two years later by another store selling dry goods, furniture and appliances, by which time the third brother, Frank, had entered the business as well. Like many of the town's businessmen, the Martins are also landlords and insurance agents. The three brothers now run the business with Arthur as managing director, Jacob and Edward having retired. Their interests thus range over diversified retail sales, pulpwood contracting, saw-milling, transportation, construction, insurance, and property.

Arthur became mayor of Focaltown in 1969, having served two terms as deputy mayor. His brother James was then President of the Chamber of Commerce, and the third brother, Frank, had been a member of the Focaltown Integrated School Board until it was disbanded. All three were members of the Lions Club, but none was actively involved in its policy making, although Arthur is a past President of the club. With the exception of James, who, except when the interests of the family business dictate otherwise, has tired to steer a middle course in the inter-group conflict, the brothers were clearly identifiable with the People's Group. Arthur, as the eldest son of the dynasty (cf. Matthews, 1970, 224) and incumbent of the culturally legitimate role of mayor, was the Group's most prestigious member. Frank was a peripheral activist.

Their father, Edward, was, until the advent of the Sophisticates, the acknowledged authority of the town. Arthur describes his dominance in these terms:

I don't mean to be boastful about it, but we were kings. It was a typical Newfoundland outport, and there's usually one king in each of them. During those years it was my father. He either started most of the organisations or played a leading part in them.

Clearly, the basis of his father's political predominance was his mercantile dominion:

... over the years, I suppose for—well—twenty or thirty years, Focaltown was this firm and vice versa. You know, I mean if they worked, they worked here; and there was no cash so they dealt here—it was sort of a captive thing ...

The family thus built obligations through credit transactions and provided the main intra-community source of employment. The townspeople's financial obligations and cultural predispositions reinforced their inclination to political deference and reluctance to accept positions of leadership and responsibility (cf. Evans, 1966, Part II, 6), creating a leadership vacuum. With his economic power and consequent independence forming a vital resource, the merchant was able to monopolise leadership roles in the community. This pragmatic use of credit obligations to build political power was a ubiquitous phenomenon of the Newfoundland outport (see Lodge, 1939, 55, 57; McLintock, 1941, 121; Smith, 1968, 15). In Focaltown his dominance was so well-entrenched that it could not—and would not—be challenged from within the community. But he was to be overtaken, first politically and then commercially, by community immigrants. The challenge to his authority, which was effective, came to his position as Chairman of the United Church School Board. The source of the challenge, Wayne Eaton, whom I regard as the Sophisticates' leader, tells the story. I quote it at length because it contains several key clues to the contemporary politics of Focaltown's leadership:

Mr Edward Martin . . . went to Florida in the winter and there were no meetings of the School Board held when he was away. They were building a $90,000 church and when I was invited to attend a Loyalty dinner as a member, as an adherent to the United Church, I remember going along and listening and coming away saying, 'Well, gentlemen, I admire the energies you are putting into building a church but I just wish to hell you had a little more concern for the education of the youth. You can praise God anywhere if you want to, but you've got to have good classrooms and facilities for the kids to get an education. So I started a campaign, not against the church, but for education. And through the Lions Club we initiated the first effort to get the amalgamation of the school system . . . The School Board decided to add two or three to its membership, and I was one of them. We got a project launched to add to the school's building, and after about six months of being associated with the Board, I made a motion, only to be told by the chairman (Edward Martin) that I couldn't make it because I wasn't a member—I was only in an assisting capacity, not as a full member of the Board. You can imagine my reaction to it. My reaction was such that Mr Edward Martin spent a week in bed afterwards and Arthur called on me to discuss it. I made no apology at all. I told Arthur the day was come when his father had to recognise that *he* didn't run the town any more, that the need of the children was far greater than the need for his father to retain the leadership he had. And I was quite frank with him about it. A congregational meeting was called and the Board was thrown out completely and there was a whole new group nominated at that meeting. We met immediately afterwards and set up a new Board and I was elected as chairman . . .

The first of the clues is the enduring rivalry of the Martins and Wayne Eaton—which has extended from the political into the commercial sphere. The second is the individualistic nature of the organisational activities of the People's Group as evident both in the statement that the School Board ceased functioning when their chief spokesman was absent and in the apparent ease with which their authority was overthrown—due, clearly, to their lack of organisational cohesiveness. The third was the Sophisticates' use of the—then embryonic—Lions Club to launch their educational campaign, rather than the more institutionally appropriate organisation of the School Board. Unable to gain admission to power in existing institutions, the Sophisticates, characteristically, created new ones.

A fourth clue is the choice of education as the issue on which the active confrontation should commence. It is no coincidence that the Sophisticates have always been associated with educational policy in Focaltown, for it lends substance to their meritocratic myths. These points will be taken up later on. Suffice it to note for now that the nature of the confrontation between the merchant and acknowledged leader, on the one hand, and the upstart newcomer on the other, may well explain the intensity of feeling in the conflict between the associates of the traditional leadership—Arthur Martin and the other People's Group activists—and the Sophisticates.

The mercantile pre-eminence of the Martins in Focaltown was unusual in that it rested on more complex bases than the fishery. Typically in Newfoundland, the viability of the outport was dependent solely on the cod fishery. Without the merchant, as the source of supplies and the outlet for the catch, the fishery could not be prosecuted. Dealings between the merchant and fishermen were always in credit. The merchant outfitted the fisherman, and 'sold' him basic subsistence goods for the winter; having no cash, the fisherman paid off part of this debt with the next season's catch. The malleability of the landing price for cod was such that it was virtually impossible—certainly very rare—for the fisherman to pay off his debt in full (cf. Prowse, 1895, 379–80; Feltham, 1959, 12 ff.). Of course, the local merchant was often as vulnerable as the fisherman: he dealt in credit with *his* suppliers in St John's, so that if the catch failed, so—frequently—did he.

The inshore fishery in Newfoundland has gradually declined, owing to a variety of factors: the catches themselves have been unreliable, the market for Newfoundland fish has changed, and the Provincial government deliberately decided that, in any case, it was not compatible with the industrial development which was to follow Confederation. With the decline, and with the introduction of cash from welfare payments, the bases of the merchant's monopoly were considerably weakened. In many of the smaller communities the merchant disappeared altogether. In others he has had to engage in various adaptive strategies.

But in Focaltown merchants had to engage in adaptive strategies very much sooner. Fish was never the rationale for the community's existence, but while the herring fishery did briefly flourish it provided the Martins with the opportunity to exploit the credit system and lay the foundations of their business. When economic activity reverted to the woods, Edward Martin accordingly extended the credit system there, and refused to pay his men in cash. They could redeem their wage-tokens only at his store. It was the threat to his captivity of this clientele, posed by Eaton's intention to pay *his* men in cash, that explains Martin's early hostility to Eaton, and his efforts to keep Eaton 'out of town'. But, of course, cash could only be resisted for so long, and eventually the Martins were forced to compete as a retail outlet. Whilst they are still large employers, they have watched their mercantile supremacy slip away to the greater commercial energies of Wayne Eaton. Here is one of the crucial differences between them: the

Martins are prominent in Focaltown's business affairs, still second only to Eaton. But they do not present an *entrepreneurial* image. They appear as reluctant innovators. And this apparent commercial reticence redounds to their political advantage. They are still spoken of as 'merchants'. Eaton, on the other hand, is called by the modern term 'businessman', signifying his innovative aggressiveness. Despite the present diversification of their business, the Martins still maintain the *visage* of the traditional merchant. They still sit in their cramped offices, separated only by the counter from the hardware store, and manage to preserve the customary role of the store as casual meeting place. Eaton, on the other hand, occupies a smart, modern, carpeted office, barricaded by secretaries and receptionists. Despite, also, the Martins' associations with the credit system, their 'traditional' behaviour has enabled them to retain the sympathy of the local consumer; it is the cash innovators who are seen as 'sharks'.

All of this suggests the success with which the Martins have managed to carry over the legitimacy which traditionally attached to the merchant into their own, rather different situations. The strategy is one which has been deliberately pursued by Arthur Martin and which points logically to cultural-extension over a range of associated myths. What has clearly been lost, though, is their predominance over the town's governmental and organisational life. In this respect they may have retained their legitimacy, but have manifestly lost the initiative.

Eaton's account of his conflict with Edward Martin itself suggests the extent to which the latter was politically predominant. But the career of the second People's Group activist provides a further indication.

Thomas Rodgers was, until his retirement, woods superintendent for the Martins, having worked his way steadily up the logging hierarchy. A forceful personality by any standards, he was Edward Martin's 'nominee' for the mayoralty, which he held for twenty years from the time of the town's initial incorporation.[3] He was, therefore, the beneficiary of two 'residual' sources of legitimacy: his association with the traditional leadership—the Martins; and his incumbency of the mayoralty. Following his retirement he bought a motel a few miles outside town which is managed by his son.

One of the ascriptive features of political legitimacy in Newfoundland may, perhaps, best be described as 'legitimacy by incumbency, or association'. One dimension of this is that the longer you occupy a 'legitimated' role or office, the greater the legitimacy of *your* incumbency (and, concomitantly, the *less* legitimate is challenge to or criticism of your incumbency). The individual becomes legitimate as an individual by association with a legitimated role. It is, perhaps, this phenomenon which helps to explain political longevity in the Province. Joe Smallwood, for example, was premier for an uninterrupted term of twenty-two years. There are many cases, at various levels of government, of such resilience, not least, of course, being that of Thomas Rodgers himself. The extension of legitimacy to an individual by virtue of his association with a legitimated role is clearly a contextual phenomenon of great assistance of myth managers, as they seek to legitimate themselves through association with a set of valued principles. It is a compatibility which both Smallwood and, imitatively, Rodgers exploited to great effect, by using the association almost in reverse—the second dimension. Their personal 'legitimacies' became so great that, at their peaks, the fact of their sponsorship of or support for some innovation was generally sufficient to accord it legitimacy. In other words, legitimacy could also be extended from the individual to the structure (or to another individual). Thus, for example, the institution of a town council in Focaltown was accepted relatively quickly because of Rodgers' active participation within it. Similarly, the new 'participatory' Liberal party organisations anathema to traditional modes of political behaviour in Newfoundland acquired legitimacy only when Smallwood sponsored them in 1968-9, following his announced intention to retire from office. The same consideration of associative legitimacy brought Rodgers, on one of his then rare public appearances, to the founding meeting of the Herring Bay party branch.

This phenomenon accounts also for the ways in which Smallwood and outport leaders like Rodgers 'borrow' legitimacy from each other, by constantly demonstrating their association, a technique which Smallwood perfected during the Confederation campaign. When, for example, Focaltown's impressive new amalgamated high school was to be opened officially and named after Rodgers, the premier did not miss the opportunity of the ceremony—four months before a general election—to express the intimacy of his relationship with and the extent of his regard for Thomas Rodgers:

Perhaps more than any other man in the history of Focaltown he has served the community and helped to make it the lovely progressive growing town that it is tonight. A great son of Newfoundland ... *He has been my friend longer than anyone else in Focaltown* ...[4]

In like manner, and in common with the third member of the People's Group, to be introduced shortly, Rodgers' strategy of self-legitimisation was based on continual expression of his association with Smallwood. He has filled a role which, for reasons I discuss later, is best described as a would-be broker for Smallwood, mediating between Focaltown and the surrounding communities, and the premier. It is questionable whether Smallwood actually required a broker for the allocation of patronage, but I would suggest four reasons for his pragmatic 'maintenance' of *self-appointed* or *would-be* brokers. Firstly, to provide local organisation for election purposes, in the absence of local party organisations. Secondly, to create the impression of devoluted power—which may also explain his creation of local party organisations after the resources of patronage had either been expended or become too expensive. Thirdly, if he decided to withhold his patronage, for whatever reason, the local brokers could be made into scapegoats: they could be left to reap the blame from the community for having performed their self-proclaimed brokerage functions inadequately, and Smallwood's image could thus remain unimpaired. And fourthly, of course, there are always private and intra-party battles to be fought, and the prospect of committed and possibly influential local supporters is one that no politician so astute as Smallwood would take lightly. Examples of the efficacy of his local brokers in this respect will be discussed later on. Suffice it to note for the time being that Thomas Rodgers has effectively run the premier's campaigns, both public and private, in the area. He has the reputation in Focaltown of being an extremely skillful politician, and successfully cultivated his image as a 'common working man' to mobilise popular support whenever it was needed. An apt example is provided by his attendance at the inaugural meeting of the Herring Bay District Liberal Association, at which he nominated his protégé for the presidency, against the opposition of a young, articulate graduate teacher. The premier was also present, rooting for the same man, and compensating for his favourite's manifestly inferior intellect by asserting that 'Liberalism lies in a man's heart rather than his head'. Thomas Rodgers slowly rose at the front of the hall to make his nominating speech, impressively dressed in what were obviously among his oldest and, uncharacteristically, shabby clothes, and proceeded to speak, lapsing frequently and deliberately into the speech of the 'bay'. His candidate won, albeit narrowly.

And the candidate, Stan Lester, is the third principal member of the People's Group. He is the owner of a hotel in the town, and a man with strong family roots in Focaltown. It is estimated that he has some two hundred kinsmen in the community, many of whom can be counted on to give him their electoral support. It was generally recognised that Lester is intent on becoming the Liberal candidate for the provincial district of Herring Bay, and much of his considerable activity around the bay was seen as directed towards this end. In his own estimation, becoming the local Member of the House of Assembly would simply legalise the *de facto* situation. Thus, he reports answering the premier's question of whether he wants the candidacy by saying, 'Why not? I might as well get a salary for doing what I'm doing now.' That statement, however, may not accurately represent the intensity of his ambition. One of the Sophisticates, and the man whom Lester regards as his most important political rival, says of him:

You always have your egos and your psychological needs to satisfy, I suppose, but nobody is coldly pragmatic about their involvement (in community affairs); nobody goes about saying 'I am going to do this so it will net me that'. With one exception. And that's Stan Lester. Stan has a long-term goal in mind, namely the candidacy for Membership of this district to replace —— as M.H.A. and I would say he spends his time every morning saying 'How can I do something that will benefit Stan Lester today?' As a result, you will find him in the forefront of a number of areas but, I would stress, solely because I feel that he's got a motive which is very selfish. I don't regard him as a community builder.

Doubtless Lester would say much the same of his detractor. Nevertheless, he admitted that he wants the nomination and claims that the premier had offered it to him. His claim may well be true, but not be a particularly significant indication of Mr Smallwood's intentions, since at least two of Lester's potential rivals also claimed to have been offered the nomination.[5] He describes the premier as a 'personal friend', and even suggested to me that he was instrumental in persuading Smallwood to seek re-election to the Liberal Party leadership. He regards himself as the prime intermediary in the area between the population of the surrounding outports and the government, and regales all who will listen with accounts of his success as a broker for some of these communities. For example, a fisherman in a nearby outport wanted the harbour light lit:

... he told me that he was waiting for this light to be lit that goes in the harbour, you see. I said, 'That's simple'. He said 'what do you mean?' I said it was just a matter of me knowing the right person. He just didn't believe that this could be done. This is something big. I just picked up the phone and called this guy in St John's and told him about this particular light and I said 'We want this lit'. ... I said 'We would like to have it lit as soon as you can get word to somebody to light it' ... It's as simple as that. This is one thing that I proved to those people. They laughed when I said, 'Well, I can have that done'. I said to them, 'If I thought there was going to be any trouble, I would ... call the Minister of Transport and that thing will be lit before the end of this month'.

He suggests that his efficacy extends beyond providing flashing lights:

You can take the Minister of Welfare. He called me this morning and he's coming here now at my request ... Since I asked him to come he agreed to come along and do whatever we want him to do.

He claims to have singlehandedly persuaded the Government to grant one community municipal status, to make water systems available to two others, to provide vital constructional modifications during the paving of Focaltown's access road to the Trans-Canada Highway, and to finance a $300,000 extension to Focaltown's hospital. None of the Sophisticates would acknowledge his instrumentality in any of these endeavours. Neither, as the opinion quoted above demonstrates, would they credit his proclaimed lack of self-interest:

... a hundred people have said to me, 'Well, what are you getting out of this and what kind of salary are you being paid?' or some sort of thing like this. I say to them, 'If you knew what this is costing me personally out of my own pocket, you would be frightened stiff. This costs me literally hundreds of dollars a year'. Well ... possibly there are a lot of other people that benefit more from my efforts than I do myself.

He does not hesitate, however, to emphasise—publicly and privately—how much effort he does put into his local activities.

It is apparent that he vastly overestimates his support at both governmental and popular levels. On the occasions when he has chosen to test his electoral support he has had very moderate success. His electoral performance tends to confirm Bailey's scepticism of the broker's attempt to change his status through the evocation of his—overestimated—public support (cf. Bailey, 1969, 167–74). He has run three times for election to the town council. He was unsuccessful in his first two attempts—being defeated on the second occasion at a by-election by a Sophisticate. On his third try he told me that he anticipated topping the poll, but in fact came seventh, thereby gaining the last seat on council. His only real electoral successes—to the presidency of the Herring Bay District Liberal Association, and as Herring Bay delegate to the national Liberal leadership convention—demanded the active, and devious, intervention of both the premier and Thomas Rodgers, and in the first case, also of the weather which prevented twelve of his opponent's supporters from being present. There is no doubt that the premier and his associates are aware of his lack of influence, and I would argue that their reasons for maintaining him in his broker's image are to be found among the four I suggested earlier. In support of that argument it may be noted that, with an executive drawn almost entirely from the Pentecostal congregation, he chaired the Herring Bay 'Action-for-Joey Committee' in the Liberal leadership contest.[6]

Apart from his membership of the town council Lester belongs to the Lions Club, but has always been excluded from an executive position in it, and is—by right—a member of the Chamber of Commerce. He explains away his somewhat passive roles in these organisations by asserting the greater efficacy of individual, as opposed to organisational behaviour. This argument, although obscuring the possibility that his non-involvement is the consequence of wills other than his own, is consistent with the mythic political style of the People's Group activists, as will become evident in the course of this essay. Their identities, as myth managers are invariably personalised rather than mediated by their organisational structures. Arthur Martin is thus identified as the head of the Martin family, rather than as chief spokesman of the town council; Rodgers' populism identifies him in individualistic terms, rather than in terms of his association with the various institutions in which he was instrumental. Much of Lester's strategy is directed towards demonstrating his independence from the various organisations of the town. In this way he dissociates himself from their predominantly 'middle-class' members, and identifies himself with the rural proletariat. Each of these three guises has concomitant strategic procedures governing the ways in which the myth managers present themselves to their followings—their responses to deference, the use of forms of address, the formulation of political appeals, and so on. I discuss these in some detail in the chapters which follow. But their sensitivity to these neo-ritualistic procedures, and their entitlement to use them—given by their contrived identities—constitute important tactical political resources which are denied to the Sophisticates. In terms of the traditional cultural values, the People's Group activists, in this respect, know how to act out their leadership roles; the Sophisticates lack this knowledge, and also the cultural entitlement to assume the roles. They therefore redefine them and attempt to create a new and appropriate set of interpersonal rituals in which the use of organisational identity and office figures prominently.

Despite Stan Lester's obvious delusions, his inclusion among the major activists is imperative. In the first place he has managed to establish an image as an effective broker in some of the nearby outports, albeit the smaller ones. There was also some indication that although not a member, he was beginning to establish a support base in the local Pentecostal congregation; and, given the numerical importance of the denomination in Focaltown, that has some significance. It did not necessarily increase his utility to Smallwood since the support of members of the Pentecostal congregation for Lester derives from his being Smallwood's man: they did not require Lester's persuasion to support Smallwood. But it does give him an important resource in any intra-party contest in which he might become involved, and may have increased his electoral strength as a candidate for the town council. Secondly, anticipation of his involvement in local issues frequently provides the Sophisticates with additional reasons for pursuing contemplated courses of action. When, for example, the local newspaper was to change hands, one of the Sophisticates, aware of Lester's desire to buy it, capitalised on his close relationship with the retiring owner by persuading her of the folly of selling it to Lester, and subsequently bought it himself at a much reduced price. There is little doubt that this Sophisticate sought ownership of the newspaper both as a propaganda instrument for himself and as a business investment, but scoring a point off Lester—who perceives him as a political rival—and depriving him of an important medium for his own propaganda provided a powerful and explicit incentive. It also served as his justification to his somewhat suspicious Sophisticate colleagues. Similarly, whilst their establishment of the Herring Bay Economic Development Association was obviously motivated by anticipation of the potential benefits that a strengthened local economy would bring to them, the Sophisticates may also have seen it as a means to undermine Lester's ascendancy in the 'bay' and to acquire some legitimacy themselves. There are, indeed, any number of cases in which Stan Lester might have been a minor variable in Sophisticate decision-making but, for the most part, these have to remain in the realm of speculation. Whatever his actual importance in this respect, two of the Sophisticates—both his political rivals—do expend a great deal of concern about him.

Thirdly, he has strong associations with the traditional leadership of the community through which he has become involved with the activities of the other two main People's Group activists. He is a descendant of one of Focaltown's original families. He is related to Thomas Rodgers, who has gone to great pains to establish Lester as his protégé. And he is an old friend and drinking companion of Arthur Martin. Their relationship has commercial aspects as well, since Lester buys a great deal of the food for his hotel from the Martins' firm, giving them business worth thousands of dollars each year.

Thus there are a number of characteristics which the three People's Group activists have in common, distinguishing them from the Sophisticates. They are all associated with the traditional leadership of the community, and with the culturally legitimate institutions of leadership, such as the town council. Then, they are all identified with the *status quo* of Smallwood Liberalism, which is built on the indigenous cultural disinclination to become politically involved and equally marked inclination to defer to paternalistic authority, and on patronage. Firstly, the maintenance of 'broker' status depends partly on maintenance of the clients' belief in the need for a broker and, thus, on their dissuasion from direct political action which could make the broker redundant. Focaltown political culture does not value such action and the brokers simply reinforce this negative value. That *organisations* have only recently appeared in the outports is an indication of the negative valuation of participation and this, indeed, partly explains the People's Group's continuing attempt to conceal its organisational involvement behind individualistic and face-to-face approaches. And secondly, the maintenance of broker status depends in part both on the clients' belief in the existence of patronage to be allocated, and in their belief in the broker's proximity to the patron.[7] In their exploitation of these traditional cultural values, the People's Group becomes both culture-extending and beneficently authoritarian. A further common characteristic lies in their old-established residence in the town: they were all born within three miles of Focaltown and are thus at least second-generation residents of the locality. Apart from giving them vast and complex kinship relations in the town, old-established residence lends them legitimacy, and seems to protect them from the popular suspicions of economic self-interest in their political activity which typically attach to the Sophisticates. But most important, it has made them subject to the inculcation of the community's traditional authority values and to the constraints of its authority structure (cf. LeVine, 1960, 57, 58). I would emphatically suggest that myth managers should not be regarded as solely pragmatic in the myths they narrate; they may share the constructions of reality that they seek to impose on others through myth managment. In this regard, the People's Group activists' indigenous origins as well as their managerial strategy may incline them away from the critical, assertive organisational style of the Sophisticates.

Finally, like Mr Smallwood himself, the People's Group activists project personal images with which local citizens can readily identify, the images being those of political-cultural affinity and social familiarity. Rodgers and Lester (' . . . my heart makes up for what I haven't got in the head') identify themselves, through their populist-broker guises with the 'common man'. Arthur Martin's intimate association with the traditional mercantile community leadership, and his incumbency of the mayoralty, suit him to be the object of the customary deference of the Focaltowner. Furthermore, whilst the Newfoundland outport merchant was traditionally ascendent and, to a great extent, held the fate of the local population in his hands through the use of credit, he frequently seems to have attempted to minimise, or perhaps to *appear* to minimise, the social distance between himself and his clientele. We might note in this regard, that both Edward and Arthur Martin, though his employers and status superiors, served *under* Thomas Rodgers as deputy mayor. Edward's brother, Jacob, though a very wealthy man, dresses in the fashion of the typical outport labourer, and is 'Uncle' Jacob to the townspeople.[8] This partial equalising of status probably derives from the historical fact that the outport merchant was subject to the same fluctuations of fortune as his clients: as I said earlier, if the fishery failed, so, frequently, did he (cf. Perlin, 1972). Following Worsley's analysis, this element of apparent equalitarianism may also help to explain the historical tradition of populist politics in Newfoundland (Worsley, 1967, 164 ff.; 1970*a*, 229). Further, in his typical role as a medium for the communication of the outport's wishes and grievances, the merchant was identified with the population's interests (cf. Matthews, 1970; Iverson and Matthews, 1968).

Thus, the mode of People's Group activists' political behaviour and the issues to which they give priority apparently conform with those generated and sanctioned by traditional political culture. In this regard as well, their myth-managing style may be seen as culture-extending. I shall expand on this later on.

I would, then, reiterate the characteristics of People's Group membership as follows: identification with the traditional leadership of the community, and with Smallwoodism and traditional political values; and long-established family roots in the community.

The management of myths

THE SOPHISTICATES' GROUP

Since they rest on rather more explicit bases, the characteristics of the Sophisticate leadership are more easily stated and, to degrees which vary slightly among the individual members, may be opposed to those attributed to the People's Group.

The Sophisticate activists comprise a political elite; the bases of their ascendancy are meritocratic and organisational. They are not a totally solidary group but, because of their characteristic strategy of organisational assertiveness, tend to concert their activities to a greater degree than the People's Group. The four members of the Sophisticates' Group persistently and insistently profess an interest in the social and economic welfare of the community and publicly equate 'community spirit' with something approaching self-fulfilment, thus suggesting its intrinsic moral goodness. Their characteristic political activity thus resembles a ritual through which the mythic values of social (and moral) goodness are expressed.

They regard organisational involvement and executive responsibility as prime indicators of community spirit: they each have an average simultaneous executive membership of eight different organisations. Their proclivity to organisational activity should be contrasted with the People's Group activists' individualistic behaviour and neglect of voluntary associations. The Sophisticates' two most important organisations are the Lions Club and the Chamber of Commerce, in that order. Indeed, membership of the Lions Club is a *sine qua non* for even peripheral activists in the Sophisticates' cause. There are oligarchical features in the structure of the Lions Club—invited candidacy for membership, the probationary period for initiates, and the exclusive right of past presidents to nominate the executive—and the Sophisticates, three of whom are past presidents, make full use of them. Membership of both of these organisations is restricted to businessmen and 'professionals', and they are the primary policy-making bodies for the community. (The town council has generally only performed administrative functions.)

Community decision-making in Focaltown is thus firmly in the hands of the businessmen and, because they dominate the businessmen's organisations, is controlled by the Sophisticates. It is a situation to which they proudly admit. Their justifications are, firstly, that their financial or career successes are proof of their ability; and secondly, that as businessmen, they have a greater stake in the community than the working class. Sophisticate activism is, therefore, built on the shared characteristic of belief, firstly, in the efficacy and desirability of organisational co-operation, and secondly, in the right of elite or socially exclusive organisations to impose priorities on the community. The assertiveness and manner of their organisational activity is anathema to the traditional political culture. It explicitly rejects the primacy of the culturally legitimate institutions of ascriptively-based leadership (the traditional merchant) and electoral or public office (the Magistracy, town council, etc.). It is, therefore, culture-substituting.

A second common characteristic of Sophisticate activists is that they are all outsiders. This seems to be significant for three reasons. Firstly, they were less subject to the inculcation of the community's traditional authority values, and may thus have felt fewer cultural inhibitions about challenging the existing leadership. Secondly, as outsiders, they were neither financially nor politically obligated to the dominant merchant family. And thirdly, simply being outsiders and meeting the kind of resistance to their participation in community affairs that Wayne Eaton describes in his encounter with Edward Martin may well have increased their determination to break into community affairs. Wayne Eaton's proud and variously expressed credo is that if he found doors closed to him, he would simply erect others that he *could* walk through and, indeed, could close to unwanted intruders.

Eaton, whose challenge to the leadership of Edward Martin has already been described, is the leader, or principal catalyst, of the Sophisticates. A highly successful businessman, he moved to Focaltown in 1955 from a nearby island where, after working for Bowaters, he had first run his own logging business, and subsequently went into business with his father—a fisherman turned general dealer and boat-builder. His first dispute with the Martins, mentioned above, dates from these days:

. . . I was quick to adopt the policy of setting up a pay roll, in those days monthly, and paying the men I employed by cash. This was almost unheard of, of course, up to that time. Locally, the only people that got paid in cash were those employed by the two paper companies (Bowaters and Anglo-Newfoundland Development) and they were privileged people, we felt. So I remember coming here to Focaltown some years after I had started doing this, and talking to the owner of the outstanding business firm here (Edward Martin), and I remember this man mention the fact that he had heard that I had been doing this and he rather thought that I was being a little bit more progressive than was necessary.

Eaton likes to remind people that he began his career as a manual worker, and attributes his purportedly good relations with his own employees to this:

I was a fisherman between my Grade 10 and my Grade 11. I was a fisherman on the schooner in Labrador. So I learnt about fishing and I slept in a bunkhole with men and got to understand human beings for what they are. Then, after that, I was a logger. I worked with Bowaters in the woods, initially on a road job with a pick and shovel. From there I went on to getting a job as assistant scaler and then a scaler . . . Then I got back into the bush work, not for the Company, but on my own, with a saw mill. So in those days I stayed with the boys . . . I drove a tractor during the day, and was a sawyer in the mill at night . . . and I usually worked fifteen or sixteen hours a day . . . . I slept in a bunkhouse with the men . . . I never sent someone to do what I wouldn't do myself. Consequently

I established a reputation for knowing what it is to work, and when I go into our logging operation today, those fellows who know me don't consider me as a businessman who was going around with a silver spoon and is just making the rounds. They know that I understand their problems. I think this is a tremendous thing; it's kept a relationship going between myself and the work force which isn't all that frequent among businessmen today.

Here he may be seen not merely to be emphasising his affinity to working men but, also, to be drawing attention to the fact that he has grown away from them. He is suggesting the meritocratic nature of his rise to power — the underlying ethic of the Sophisticates' validating myths.

His first business venture in Focaltown was as provincial agent for a brand of power saw. These power saws had not previously been used in Newfoundland and, selling in the bush and from his home, his success was immediate.[9] In the meantime he acquired some land cheaply on the outskirts of town, which he developed into a valuable sand and gravel quarry. Having towed his house into the centre of town—'We had an establishment on Main Street!'—he converted part of it into a shop selling both power saws and domestic appliances. Two years later he sold the power saw agency at a large profit which he used to start a transport enterprise hauling heavy equipment, and a pulpwood business—which became the largest of its kind in the Province. In 1960, with business booming, he added road and building construction to his growing empire, and now operates all over Newfoundland. He also began selling building supplies. Later he bought an industrial supply company and acquired a very lucrative agency for explosives for which he had a provincial monopoly. When I was in Focaltown he was planning the establishment of a $2½ million linerboard and chip mill. That had not come to fruition by the end of my fieldwork. During the summer he employed up to 230 men, dropping to 130 in the winter. His power in the local economy is thus beyond question.

A comparable success story can be told about the second member of the Sophisticate Group, Donald Farrar. He grew up in rather poor circumstances, but with some help from the Salvation Army he graduated from high school and Salvation Army College, and then went to Focaltown for a short time as a Salvation Army officer. He left to attend university and, while an undergraduate, successfully founded a newspaper for Newfoundland teachers. He went on to the United States to do graduate work, and then returned to Focaltown as Principal of the Salvation Army High School. In 1965, at the age of twenty-seven, he became Principal of the new amalgamated high school, and four years later was appointed Superintendent of the Herring Bay Consolidated School Board, a position which, with a short break, he has held since. He had in the meantime established himself provincially as a figure of political importance. For one year he published the local newspaper, and later owned a printing business and some local property. Like Eaton, Farrar identified each of the four Sophisticates as being the men who 'run the town', and was explicit about his own role:

I am not involved in the social elite,[10] but I think you will find that I am very definitely involved in the political elite, if we may coin that term . . . Politically, I get consulted on just about any decision. If some new development takes place . . . I get a call pretty quickly.

He is not exaggerating. Most frequently he was 'mobilised' by Eaton, with whom he talked at length several times weekly. But he was also known as an extremely efficient and energetic administrator who would, for whatever reason, assume organisational responsibilities. In this regard he was frequently consulted by the then mayor (Arthur Martin's predecessor) and the magistrate.[11] During the latter stages of my fieldwork he became, increasingly, the instigator in locally-based activities, assuming Eaton's catalytic role. He, of course, did not suffer the same degree of exclusion from local politics that Wayne Eaton initially experienced, since by the time he settled in Focaltown the new structures of organisational politics had become fairly well established.

The two other Sophisticates, Ivan Lush and John Whiteway, have had less spectacular careers. Ivan Lush owns the largest of the local garages and operates a lucrative school bus service; and John Whiteway, after retiring from the Newfoundland Ranger Force when the Royal Canadian Mounted Police took over police duties in the Province, settled in Focaltown—where he had been stationed for a time—and started a carpentry, building supply, and construction business, which later ran into some difficulty as a result of the competition of Eaton's much larger and more efficient business.

Both Lush and Whiteway are different in important respects from Eaton and Farrar. They have, firstly, greater personal popularity. Ivan Lush is an aggressively extroverted man with a large circle of drinking and curling companions. Whiteway's popularity derives partly from his wide acquaintance with the older generation of the local population gained during his days in the Ranger Force—an acquaintance which has given him a somewhat greater knowledge of the local political idiom than his Sophisticate colleagues. In neither case, though, should their popular following be exaggerated for it does not extend very far. Secondly, they have both been members of the town council. There are circumstantial reasons which explain their electoral successes. Lush was first elected at a by-election against the opposition of Stan Lester who, for reasons I have already mentioned, was probably more help than hindrance to Lush's candidacy. At the next general election of the council, Lush ran an intensive campaign with the explicit aim of topping the poll and thus gaining the mayoralty. He did not succeed and, indeed, his re-election may be explained by an obviously sectarian vote (see chapter 5 below)—

56 The management of myths

he was one of only a few viable candidates not actively associated with Pentecostal support—and by the residual legitimacy which attached to him as a serving member of council. John Whiteway served on early councils, which were nominated virtually single-handedly by Edward Martin, before the People's Group–Sophisticate conflict had emerged.

These differences, however, are obscured by the greater similarities of strategy, ideology, and myth-managing styles which obtain between the four members of the group. They all identify each other as intimate associates in the community's leadership and exploit their alliance.

Table 1. Past and present executive membership of policy-making and service organisations in Focaltown

	Sophisticates				People's Group		
	Eaton	Farrar*	Lush	Whiteway	Martin	Rodgers	Lester
Lions Club	X	X	X	X	X		
Chamber of Commerce	X	X	X	X			
Town council			X	X	X	X	X
School Board*	X		X	X	X		
Economic Development Association	X	X		X			
Volunteer Fire Brigade			X	X			
District party associations		X	X	X			X

* Farrar's position, first as Principal, and then as Superintendent, prohibits him from appointment to the School Board

Unlike the People's Group activists, all four of the Sophisticates are intensively involved in organisational activity at the community, provincial, and, in two cases, national levels. (Table I compares the past and present executive memberships held by People's Group and Sophisticate activists in the most important political and service organisations in Focaltown.) Wayne Eaton was a past President of both the Lions Club and the Chamber of Commerce, founding President of the Herring Bay Economic Development Association, past Chairman of the Focaltown Amalgamated School Board, Newfoundland Governor of the Atlantic Provinces Economic Council, Vice-President of the Canadian Cancer Society,[12] Chairman of the Red Cross Committee and so on and on. Donald Farrar was President of the Herring Bay Economic Development Association, Vice-President of the Chamber of Commerce, and an ex-executive member of the Lions Club, Past President of the Newfoundland Teachers' Association and Councillor of the Canadian Teachers' Federation, was a Vice-President of the provincial Liberal Party, and was a leading campaign organiser for one of Smallwood's main opponents in the Liberal leadership contest. Ivan Lush was, as mentioned, a town councillor serving his second term (and was concerned, on council, with protecting Sophisticate 'interests'), was President of the district Progressive Conservative Association and had twice been the district's Progressive Conservative candidate for the provincial legislature, a past President of the Lions Club, and retired Chief of the Volunteer Fire Brigade.[13] And John Whiteway was the founding President of both the Lions Club and the Chamber of Commerce, an ex-Councillor, twice Progressive Conservative candidate for the Provincial riding, retired Chief of the Volunteer Fire Brigade, a former member of the School Board and Library Board, and Vice-President of the Economic Development Association.

The Sophisticates, then, are businessmen and organisers. Their businesses —and Farrar's career—are clearly founded in somewhat different circumstances from those of the People's Group. (A view of the Sophisticates as *political* entrepreneurs will be discussed later.) All of them are built on the rapid economic modernisation that has taken place in Newfoundland since Confederation. The commercial enterprises are symptomatic of a post-credit, capitalistic economy, whilst Farrar's career must be seen within the context of an educational system which in part, increases mobility in the class system. They are, essentially, the 'bay men' who have 'made good'. And importantly, in making good, they have eliminated the commercial and political pre-eminence of the traditional merchant. Moreover, in creating organisations which smack of modernity, and which neutralise the effective power of the 'legitimate' institutions of leadership, they have challenged and rejected the traditional figures and modes of leadership. It is this common rejection of traditional politics which forms their third shared characteristic.

As I have already suggested, the dividing line between pragmatism and ideology as motivating elements of their rejection of traditional values is problematic. But what is clear is, firstly, that the characteristics mentioned disqualify them from participation in People's Group—or culturally legitimate—modes of political activism, so they resort to the development of their own exclusive idioms. Secondly, the divergence of characteristics between the groups complements and, perhaps, reinforces their respective orientations to different mythical systems of order. In these respects, the political milieu, by providing both the normative inclination and the exigencies of competition, 'forces' the Sophisticates to their stance of strategic opposition. This suggests that the groups are, to some extent, led to their situation of conflict—the oppositional types are created—*by the fact of their interaction*. It may be argued that, as a general rule, this phenomenon of the definition of oppositions through interaction is present in those political confrontations in which it is the *incumbency* of *given* statuses (horizontal change), rather than the very existence of those differentiated statuses (vertical change) which is at issue. In Focaltown the dispute between the activists does not concern the fact or desirability of elite leadership. The point of difference is which particular group of individuals in the leadership can legitimate their roles. It is, then, the scarcity of legitimacy—as a valued resource—which accentuates and even, to some extent, produces the differences between the strategic approaches to its acquisition, and the differentiating myths may follow as a rationalisation of this conflict. The mediating effect of interaction, therefore, makes it difficult, if not impossible, to determine whether the myths are the source or the product of the conflict, although it does account for the maintenance of idiomatic and mythic dualism among the leadership. Thus, in Focaltown, the traditional institutions go on side by side the new structures, still retaining salience for many of the population. And hence the competition for legitimacy.

It will be evident from the foregoing description of the Sophisticate activists that, unlike the People's Group, they did not support Premier Smallwood, and their rejection of him is consistent with their general rejection of traditional political values. Both Ivan Lush and John Whiteway are active in the Progressive Conservative Party, and Donald Farrar was very prominently involved in the campaign of one of Mr Smallwood's opponents for the Liberal leadership—who subsequently joined the Conservative Party. Rather like Arthur Martin, Wayne Eaton puts his business interests before his political preferences, and makes somewhat less noise than his associates about those preferences. He has indicated, however, his predilection for the entrepreneurial 'middle class' politicians, who rose to prominence as opponents of Smallwood within the Liberal Party.[14] In this respect as well, then, the Sophisticates appear as the seekers of change.

Again in contrast to the People's Group activists, the prestige of the Sophisticates rests on their images as 'achievers', and in these images their public and private careers are not differentiated. Indeed, much of the resentment which attaches to them as politicians derives from their business or professional activities. It is presumably because such role distinctions are not made in respect of the Sophisticates taht they are so much more frequently the targets for accusations of self-seeking in their community affairs than their opponents. On the other hand, the leadership performances of People's Group activists, through whichever roles they are conducted, are evaluated independently of their business or career fortunes. The Sophisticates' leadership roles are largely ones they created for themselves, justifying their incumbency of them by their career successes. If those careers should fail, their prestige as community leaders would probably disappear—as had tended to be the case with John Whiteway—as would whatever legitimacy they possess. To a considerable extent Sophisticate careers, and particularly those of Wayne Eaton and Donald Farrar, are dependent on both the image and the economic strength of Focaltown. Eaton sees his business, which operates on a Province-wide scale, as being particularly sensitive to Focaltown's image, and he explains his energetic promotion and representation of its organisations outside the community as part of his attempt to portray Focaltown as a thrusting, vital economic centre. Indeed, as a result of the influence of its Chamber of Commerce, the community calls itself 'The Boom Town of the North', 'The Town that has Everything', and 'The Industrial Heart of Herring Bay'.[15]

It seems probable that the credibility in St John's of Eaton and Farrar as Provincial figures, owes something to the impression of Focaltown that they have created through their organisations. As Eaton says,

... The [Lions] Club has been promoted outside Focaltown. It's got public relations value. I've done a P.R. job ... it has fallen to my lot, if you like, to be the one to promote the community and the Club outside of Focaltown. *By nature of my business and my association with other activities* in the Province, I have always been promoting the Lions Club and Focaltown.

There is, then, an instrumentality to Sophisticate activity which, combined with their commercial activities and non-Focaltown origins, makes them susceptible to accusations of economic self-interest. Indeed, as we shall see, these accusations are not always unjustified.

The characteristic activity of the Sophisticate group may thus be seen to differ from that of the People's Group, in that it is organisationally based on unlegitimated and exclusive institutions, and informed by situationally 'new' values. The nature of such values, the goals of their activity, and the characteristic political behaviour of the Sophisticates through which they are expressed will be discussed in the chapters which follow.

The opposing characteristics of People's Group and Sophisticate membership may be tabulated, then, as follows:

	People's Group	*Sophisticates*
(a)	Indigenous	Immigrants
(b)	Pro-Smallwood	Anti-Smallwood
(c)	Associated with traditional community leadership	Opposed to traditional community leadership
(d)	Traditional political values	'New' political values
(e)	Personal involvement	Organisational involvement

NOTES TO CHAPTER THREE

[1] There is a Paretan dimension to this argument: oligarchic achievers have a tendency to become ascriptive over time.

[2] Indeed, at one stage of my fieldwork, I found that two Sophisticates were attempting to use me as a source of information on the other's surreptitious activities and opinions.

[3] The mayor of Newfoundland municipalities is elected by councillors from their own number for the four-year life of the council. The convention in Focaltown has been for the councillor with the highest number of votes to become mayor, although this was not followed in 1969.

[4] *Focaltown News*, 1 December 1965.

[5] None of these men obtained the nomination. It finally went to a minister in Smallwood's government who had previously represented a nearby district.

[6] Most legislative districts of the Province had organisational committees working for the two major candidates, Premier Smallwood and John Crosbie. Their task, basically, was to enrol party members, in the hope that they would support convention delegates pledged to their candidate; and to exploit the peculiar conditions of the locality to ensure the election of their slate of delegates. In this latter regard, the means employed ranged from the conventional—canvassing, acquiring sponsors of high prestige, and fund-raising—to the distinctly devious: in Herring Bay all the buses in the region were hired by Smallwood's group, so that their opponents had no means of bringing their supporters in to the nominating meetings in Focaltown. In other and more volatile parts of the Province there were reports of telephones being tapped, contracts and liquor licences promised, intimidation, and vast amounts of money changing hands.

[7] I refer here to typical structures of brokerage as they are found in Herring Bay. Discussion of the *concept* of broker is reserved until later.

[8] Elderly men who are held in particular affection in Focaltown are frequently called 'Uncle'. It is a rare and jealous honour reserved for very few. It would certainly not extend to Edward Martin ('Mr Edward'), whose style is quite different. Jacob still lives permanently in Focaltown; Edward spends most of the year in Florida.

[9] Eaton found his original market for power saws among loggers. They were generally paid on piece-rate, and the mechanical saw enabled them to increase their output considerably. (Of course, it also reduced the number of jobs available in the woods, now tightly controlled by the unions through a somewhat devious probationary scheme.) Later they were bought by ordinary householders as a welcome aid to the onerous and monotonous chore of sawing logs for the wood stove. Prior to the installation of electricity in Herring Bay, completed only in the late 1960s, wood was used almost everywhere for cooking and heating fuel. The potential sales for the power saw were, consequently, enormous.

[10] He explains his apparent exclusion from the 'social elite' on the grounds of his bachelorhood. As an unmarried man he cannot reciprocate with invitations to his home. Among middle-class Focaltown couples, it is the wives' friendships which tend to determine visiting relationships. The common pastime in such predominantly housebound entertaining is cardplaying. Farrar, perhaps as a result of his days as a Salvation Army officer, did not gamble and drank very little alcohol.

[11] Both these men belong to the group I call the 'Legitimisers' (see p. 37, n. 10 above). I discuss them in greater detail later.

[12] These last two positions should not be taken as an indication of Eaton's national standing. They are largely honorific offices to which he was nominated *from Newfoundland*, and they are, thus, more accurately seen as proof of his activity in the *provincial* context.

[13] The Volunteer Fire Brigade does, indeed, provide fire-fighting services, should they be required. But, in Focaltown, its primary significance is as a fund-raising organisation for various non-local charities. It is composed almost exclusively of 'middle-class' organisational activists, anxious to demonstrate the Lions' ethic of 'community service'. Executive office in the Volunteer Fire Brigade appears to be an invariable stepping-stone to high office in the Lions.

[14] These dissident Liberals, having failed to defeat Smallwood at the leadership convention in 1969, joined and revivified the Progressive Conservative Party which at present forms the provincial government.

[15] *Who's Who in Newfoundland and Labrador*, St John's, 1967. Also *Nearby Town Journal*, 1964.

CHAPTER FOUR

The political objectives of myth management in Focaltown

The political objectives of each set of activists may be stated quite simply: the *raison d'être* of the People's Group is to preserve the appearance of the political *status quo*; the object of Sophisticate endeavour is to demolish the 'traditional' structures of community leadership, and replace them with 'modernistic' structures.

This general dichotomy of the culture-extending behaviour of the People's Group and the culture-substituting behaviour of the Sophisticates, remains constant through the broad range of issues to which the opposing groups give their attention. Indeed, even in the few examples already used, we have noted it in the commercial sphere (Edward Martin's reaction to Wayne Eaton's cash payroll) as well as in the 'decisional' and governmental. The dichotomy, as should now be evident, is one of commitment to kinds of change, as well as one of strategy. It will become clear, however, that neither group seeks to change the political order which structures relations between leaders and led, but only that which reflects relations between competing groups of leaders.

The People's Group activists seek either to maintain the appearance of the political *status quo*, or to achieve gradual change which would not disturb it to too great an extent. Their concern is to demonstrate the real or mythical continuity of past and present states. It is a strategy evident also in Smallwoodism. Prior to the establishment of the local party associations in 1968 and 1969, Smallwood maintained 'key men' in their roles as would-be brokers[1] in the outports, who sought to mediate between the outport and the government (but rarely, in Herring Bay, the reverse) and who 'processed' the information percolating into the community from the external world (cf. Paine, 1971, 21; Perlin, 1972). The role was a traditional one and, indeed, it was frequently filled by traditional incumbents—merchants and, occasionally, the clergy. When the time came that he felt he could no longer maintain his typical domination with the resources of patronage which remained at his disposal, Smallwood sought to legitimate, and, maybe, regularise, the 'broker' system by clothing it in the guise of a democratic political party: most of the leading executive positions in the new party associations were filled by people who had previously been Smallwood's 'key men' in the outports.[2] (And not surprisingly, since the party associations were formed while the Liberal leadership campaign was under way: Smallwood himself attended most of the inaugural meetings at which the executives, who would also be *ex officio* voting delegates to the Convention, were elected.)

Thus at one and the same time Smallwood institutionalised an existing system, giving it the appearance of change, and actually created some change (the executives are, after all, elected by the party membership), but gave it the appearance of consistency and continuity with the past. As I suggested, similar effects may be seen in the behaviour of the People's Group activists. Whilst Stan Lester had previously run around the Bay as a self-appointed broker, he now does so as President of the local Liberal Association. Whilst the merchant *qua* merchant would previously have spoken for the community to the government, and interpreted the government to the community, he now does so as mayor. Change in the structure and process of local leadership, as created by the People's Group activists, has meant, firstly, supplication, through slightly different channels, for new forms of patronage; and secondly, the very gradual introduction of new political structures in the attempt to provide a somewhat greater political self-sufficiency in the outports thereby reducing the pressure on the central source of patronage, and to provide structural 'evidence' of the putative new democracy of Smallwoodism.

It has been argued (Barth, 1963, 6) that successful entrepreneurial innovation may be employed empirically as a prototypical model, and thus be replicated in subsequent activities. This accurately describes the Sophisticates' patterned innovative operations in Focaltown's organisational life. Examples of such patterned behaviour in Sophisticate activity can be found both in their creation of organisations (Lions, Chamber of Commerce, Economic Development Association), and in their extra-organisational instrumentality—as in the movement to unseat the Member of the House of Assembly, to censor the editor of the *Focaltown News*, and in their initiation of proposals for a Chamber of Commerce and a stadium, all of which will be described later. It is, indeed, partly the regularity of their innovative behaviour which lends the flavour of ritual to Sophisticate legitimisation strategy. The activists conceive an idea and effectuate it either through the anonymity of an organisational 'front' or through the impersonal device of the the organisational role, constantly dressing it in the myth of 'service'.

Barth (*ibid.*) conceives the entrepreneur to be associated with 'highly seminal points of social change'. Here again the Sophisticate leaders, by their very political genesis and ideology, would appear to conform to such a model of entrepreneurialism. However, it is important to note that their strategic identities as harbingers of change belie the fact that their programme is one of conservative rationalisation rather than of radical reform. Indeed, the change which they espouse is really one of leadership style, as expressed in their legitimating myths. Thus, the characteristic philosophy of Sophisticate activity is a capitalistic ethic seeking the cultural and structural parity of Newfoundland with some idealised society of rationalism built on 'sound business sense' and offering plenty to those who display the 'right' social characteristics, which is located in that nebulous panacea of sanity and material satisfaction known only as 'The Mainland'. It is, in great measure, a reaction against Smallwoodism to which is attributed traditionalism, financial imbecility, and commercial skullduggery. Whilst Smallwood, immersed in the exaggerated rhetoric of a philosophy of change and reform, roared 'Confederation, more jobs, more schools, more roads, more hospitals', the Sophisticates, both local and provincial, retorted with rather more inhibited, almost actuarial passion, 'Per capita debt, Doyle and Shaheen,[3] net personal income, gross provincial product'.

Rhetorically, then, it is a philosophy of profit-maximisation which assumes that people will fall into line. The change that is valued is that which is held to be most conducive to profit-maximisation. As such, it is a philosophy which contrasts sharply with Smallwoodism—and, hence, with that of the People's Group activists. Where the Sophisticates seek economic expansion *per se*, Smallwood has sought it as a means of retaining and sustaining a population which was underemployed, under-housed, and even undernourished (cf. Gwyn, 1968, 34), and which now begins to recognise the disparities between 'mainland' and Newfoundland standards of living, and, indeed, the disparities within Newfoundland between the outport proletariat and the expanding urban middle class. Thus, whilst the People's Group activists associate themselves with customary styles and values of leadership, they are misunderstood if conceived to be diehard traditionalists opposed to change. They are opposed to certain *kinds* of change. But most important, they, like Smallwood, seek to defend and legitimate change by rooting it in customary practice and thus presenting it as having some continuity with a prior and, perhaps, valued state.

The values employed by the People's Group activitists to defend their resistance to Sophisticate change and their commitment to their own conception of change are, then, rarely explicitly traditionalistic. The Sophisticates, though presenting modernising *visages*, preach rationalisation rather than radicalism. Both Groups represent their own attitudes as being expedient for the community, whilst each believes the other's to be reached through calculations of personal expediency.

I remarked above that the People's Group activists have, to some extent, been forced into new forms of behaviour, both by the nature of contemporary socio-economic conditions and by the exigencies of their competition with the Sophisticates. It is difficult to separate their rhetorical commitment to Smallwood's programme and defence of change from the consequences of the changes that have affected their personal situations.

It is clear, however, that they seek to assimilate change to the existing structures of leadership and to their incumbencies within them, and in this respect they reject the innovative elements of Sophisticate behaviour. Unlike the Sophisticates, they do 'talk' to a mass political following and, in so doing, interpret the political world to it (see chapter 5, below). This mediatory role, and the opportunity which it presents for legitimisation, constitutes an important political resource which is not available to the Sophisticates.

I emphasise again that the objectives of the groups' political behaviour are, respectively, to preserve and to alter the real or apparent system of local leadership, and thereby to legitimate both their respective roles in the leadership and their espousal of philosophies of societal change. The groups seek to displace each other, but not to effect a redistribution of resources between leaders and the led.

The constancy of the opposing alignments and of their respective orientations to change, will be exemplified by consideration of three different areas of public policy. The first case falls within the general area of political party allegiance. It should be remembered that of the four Sophisticates, two are active Progressive Conservatives and a third was intimately associated with an opponent of Smallwood for the Liberal leadership. Two of the People's Group activists are identified as stalwart supporters of Smallwood. It should be noted also that whilst the leaders of both groups are Liberals, and will privately discuss their attitudes to Smallwood, they refrain from public statement of their political preferences. Because of this they are courted by opposing factions at the party's provincial level, and this, in itself, enhances their roles as group leaders.

Case 1. THE GROUPS AND THE PARTY'S REPRESENTATIVE

Since he had become premier, Smallwood had followed the practice of nominating all Liberal Party candidates for the provincial House of Assembly, and usually for the (federal) House of Commons as well (cf. Gwyn, *op. cit.*, 125), himself. The Herring Bay Liberals had attempted to nominate a candidate for the provincial riding themselves, but their choice was ignored by the premier who put in his own candidate—a man very closely associated with him—who was subsequently elected. Over a period of time, the Sophisticates became thoroughly disaffected with him as a Member, and decided to take steps to secure his resignation, just at the time that he was involved in some domestic litigation. Their public complaints were that he was not adequately representing the interests of his constituents nor doing anything to enhance the image of the riding and, specifically, of Focaltown. All four of them met and decided to call a meeting of all the prominent Liberal activists in the area.

The meeting was held with twenty-three Liberals present under the chairmanship of Donald Farrar, and with Wayne Eaton as secretary, and resolved, on Thomas Rodgers' apparently unwitting proposal, to seek the Member's resignation. According to one informant, Farrar, a master of legislative procedure, had towards the end of the discussion embarked on a long account of how, in British legislatures, the substantive motion under debate is sometimes put as the motion for adjournment. Having succeeded in boring Rodgers almost to sleep, he asked for somebody to propose the adjournment. Thinking that this would simply release them all from the meeting, Rodgers eagerly volunteered. When he was informed that he had just proposed the resignation of their House of Assembly Member, he rapidly excused himself from the meeting on the pretext of having somewhere else to go. However, given the intelligence and wiles of Rodgers, it would seem a plausible hypothesis that he knew very well what he was doing, and was attempting—successfully—to bluff the Sophisticates into a public position in which they could be discredited for all to see. His motion, anyway, was passed unanimously, as was one subsequently resolving to send a cable to the Member demanding his resignation. The telegram was sent with Rodgers' name appended as prime mover of the resolution and replies eventually came from both the premier and the Member, extolling the principles of 'British Justice' and, in a reference to the legal proceedings, condemning them for 'kicking a man when he was down'. Rather than risk prejudicing the court case, they asked the Member to meet them after its conclusion, to discuss his resignation. The meeting never took place.

The Sophisticates had mounted a serious challenge to the political *status quo* and had implicated the People's Group activists. The latter, either by precedent design or, if my informant is correct, rather than court ridicule by changing their stand, sought, with the apparent support of the premier, to discredit the Sophisticates and, at the same time, to reinforce the *status quo*, on which their local ascendancy depended. Their opportunity came with the meeting called to elect a delegate to attend the national Liberal leadership convention in Ottawa. Farrar decided to seek the post and asked Thomas Rodgers for his support. Rodgers declined, saying that he intended to run himself. He then asked Stan Lester for *his* support, and Lester not only agreed, but also volunteered to second the nomination. (According to Farrar, he was not yet aware that Lester saw him as a political rival.) Prior to this, Rodgers had set about arranging the meeting, not through the usual channels of media advertising, but by sending out private notices to selected individuals. A Party member from a nearby town, who was a staunch supporter of the premier, was sent in to chair the meeting. Farrar was duly nominated; then, as expected, Rodgers was nominated but declined the nomination on the grounds of his age, and in his declining speech, proposed the nomination of Stan Lester. By what he does not deny to be a pre-arranged plan, the chairman intervened to rule the nomination out of order, thereby giving Rodgers the opportunity to complain that some young 'whippersnapper outsider' was trying to tell him—Thomas Rodgers, whom 'everyone' knew *was* 'the Liberal Party in Herring Bay'—what to do. The intention was to create sympathy for himself and his nominee by exploiting the typical deference of the Newfoundlanders to 'authority', and their sensitivity to the intrusion of outsiders (cf. Faris, 1972, *passim*), of whom Donald Farrar—like the other Sophisticates—was one. It worked. Lester received a majority of three votes. Both Farrar and Lester attribute the strategy to the premier. The People's Group had reasserted its pre-eminence in the politics of local leadership and had staved off change which, as a challenge to 'legitimate' leadership, would have been culturally repugnant. The premier had extricated himself and the Member of the House of Assembly from an embarrassing situation, for having been thus discredited, the Sophisticates could not press for the Members' resignation in the local party.

The nature of the conflict itself is not particularly important, except in so far as it illustrates the differences in the groups' styles. The conflict *is* important in that it shows the groups' respective commitments to political change to be correlated with their orientation to Smallwood and, thereby, to traditional strategies of political behaviour and, especially, legitimation. These variables are associated at the provincial level also where the 'reform conservatism' (Gwyn, *op. cit.*, 282) of the entrepreneurial politicians threw them into conflict with Smallwoodism which they, also, rationalised as lying in their differing strategies for seeking change.

CASE 2. SECTARIANISM AND THE POLITICS OF EDUCATION[4]

A second instance of policy conflict lies in the area of education. Traditionally in Newfoundland each of the religious denominations had maintained its own school system under the general curricular supervision of the government. The waste of resources was enormous. In outports with perhaps no more than thirty families adhering to two or three denominations could be found three separate schools, all operating in appalling conditions—the one-room school teaching eight grades was not untypical—with unqualified teachers and no equipment.[5] And yet, in a society of delicate religious balance, denominational 'rights' were an important political consideration (cf. Noel, 1971, 275; Perlin, *op. cit.*). The religious basis of political allegiances is traditional. One writer suggests that religious conflict was imported from Ireland, and that 'the correlation between religion and political attitudes was virtually unquestioned' Smith, 1968, 24). The religious correlates of political conflict were important in the Confederation battle, with Catholics generally voting for Responsible government, and Protestants for Confederation (cf. Perlin, 1968, *passim*; Horwood, 1969, 251, 254), and remained significant: until the 1971 election, the Tory vote was largely Catholic; Protestants overwhelmingly supported Smallwood (cf. Perlin, 1972). But in Focaltown, and in Herring Bay generally, the issue is more complex than the simple Protestant–Catholic alignments would suggest. The area is predominantly Protestant, and largely Pentecostal. I have noted already that the Pentecostal Assembly accounts for approximately 40 per cent of Focaltown's population. During the late 1960s, the Government managed to secure the agreement in principle of the Protestant denominations to amalgamate and integrate their school systems, with the important qualification that the decision to amalgamate would be the prerogative of the individual local denominational school board. This qualification was added to placate both the Catholics, whose political allegiances had traditionally been affected by their determination to protect their educational rights (cf. Harris, 1969, 259), and the Pentecostalists. The latter posed far less of a pressure group provincially, with only 4·5 per cent of Newfoundland's population in 1961 (compared with the Catholics' 35·7 per cent),[6] much of it concentrated in Herring Bay, but Smallwood went to extraordinary lengths to reassure them. One consequence was that, with rumours flying around that Crosbie—Smallwood's principal opponent for the Liberal Party leadership—would deny them their separate school facilities, the Pentecostalists of Herring Bay solidly supported the Smallwood campaign. Stan Lester has astutely exploited the Pentecostalists as a base of support, largely by capitalising on the education issue.

In certain areas of Newfoundland the Pentecostalists opted to join the integrated schemes. But in Focaltown they decided to stand alone. The principal of their local high school explained the Assembly's sensitivity to the schools question thus:

... the policy is that the school is the right hand of the church ... and we believe that in order for the right attitudes to be formed toward God and toward Christianity, the school has a great influence and we like to see that we are in a position to influence—to bring about this right influence—in the school ...

This same man was, incidentally, treasurer of the Action-for-Joey Committee, and a delegate to the leadership convention, facts which themselves may indicate that the wilful segregation of the Pentecostal schools in Focaltown is not simply rooted in the tenets of fundamentalist doctrine.

It must be recalled that the Sophisticates had first burst upon the scene, not simply as challengers to Edward Martin's chairmanship of the United Church School Board, but also as proponents, through the Lions Club, of the amalgamation of all the local schools—United Church, Salvationist, Anglican, Roman Catholic and Pentecostal. From the very start, then, they were perceived by the Pentecostal Assembly as a threat, and based their 'action for change' on education. Some ten years later the United Church, Anglican, and Salvationist schools did integrate, the Pentecostalists choosing to retain their separate system. The result of integration of the three former school boards was the construction of a high school whose facilities far exceeded those of all but the best city schools and lured a substantial number of Pentecostal parents away from their own school system.

But the resentment of the Pentecostalists is to be understood not simply in terms of their reaction to this massive display of wealth and co-operative (and Sophisticate) achievement; it must be seen also within the context of their position in the local class system.

Class distinctions in Focaltown are only now being transformed from the older and simpler divisions of ascriptive elite and mass into the more complex categories of middle and working class. Formerly status and income were publicly revealed and evaluated by *local* characteristics which were far more important elements of popular consciousness than the more common components of class identity in Western, and particularly European, society. The principal components of status were denomination and having work, and these tended to coalesce: the Pentecostal Assembly contained a larger concentration of Focaltown's unemployed than any of the other denominations.

As I have already remarked, one generally associates Pentecostalism in Focaltown with the lower end of the socio-economic scale. Family size exacerbates the Pentecostalists' economic condition: 50 per cent of my survey sample in Focaltown had between four and twelve children, and almost half of these were Pentecostal families. In the Focaltown context, then, Pentecostalism was associated with extreme hardship caused by a tendency to large families and either to very badly paid employment, or to no employment at all. Such characteristics acquire a fresh cogency in a society which is suddenly invaded by the values of an exaggerated materialism after a long history of deprivation and, often, near-destitution. To the rest of the population, therefore, and particularly to the children, Pentecostalism implied definitely inferior status. From my conversations with non-Pentecostal children it became clear that a primary means of organising their social worlds was into the Pentecostal and the non-Pentecostal. The only other pair of oppositions which approached it in importance was whether or not one was a Newfoundlander. So far as these children were concerned, to be Pentecostal was to have a spoiled identity (Goffman, 1968).[7]

The social correlates of denomination therefore underline the antagonisms which were traditionally associated with doctrinal difference. The Pentecostalists saw their under-privileged position dramatically highlighted by the construction and facilities of the new amalgamated high school. The activity of the Sophisticates in the project served to emphasise the Assembly's identification of its political enemies. The new school bore everywhere the imprint of Sophisticate involvement. The Sophisticates had initiated the issue of Amalgamation; Wayne Eaton's company had built the school and he later became chairman of the school board; Donald Farrar was its principal; Ivan Lush had the school bus contract; the swimming pool and ice rink were provided largely out of funds raised by the Lions; even the school bus shelters distributed through the town were built by the Lions Club. In the face of all this endeavour the Pentecostal Assembly sought consolation and offered succour to other victims of Sophisticate might.

It found one. Stan Lester nailed an inscribed plaque to the door of the Pentecostal elementary school (which was located close to his hotel), attesting to the exemplary behaviour of its students. And when, almost simultaneously, Farrar was appointed Superintendent of the new Herring Bay Consolidated School Board, and a further $450,000 extension to Focaltown's amalgamated high school was announced, Lester really went to work. He set off on a tour of Herring Bay, armed with photographs of some very dilapidated local schools, insinuating that Farrar had used his position as President of the Newfoundland Teachers' Association, and Vice-President of the Liberal Party, to get sanction for the extension to Focaltown's school. He followed through by sending a telegram to the Minister of Education, purportedly on behalf of the Herring Bay Liberal Association (although the issue was never raised in either general or executive meetings of the Association). The telegram 'deplored' the extension as an 'outrageous expenditure' by the school board, and went on to 'condemn' the appointment to the superintendency of Farrar who, 'we feel', was responsible for this 'extravagant' expenditure. It ended by arguing that the expenditure would be at the expense of small surrounding outports. In fact many of these communities send their children to the Focaltown high school. Lester's appeal fell on deaf ears. He then proceeded to issue accusations against members of the school board and specifically its Sophisticate associates. He accused the board of embezzling $30,000. He accused it of skullduggery in awarding the contract for the extension to Eaton's company, despite a lower bid, and in giving Ivan Lush a school bus contract worth $4,000 more than that given to the second contractor in respect of less work. Finally he accused Farrar of using school board money to travel round the Province on his Teachers' Association duties.

I am not in a position to say whether there was any justification for these accusations, although I do know that Stan Lester subsequently withdrew them, under some pressure. A more important matter for the purposes at hand is that the information on which the accusations were supposedly based was given to Lester by a peripheral activist of the People's Group, Frank Martin—Arthur's brother, and youngest son of Edward whom Eaton had deposed fourteen years earlier. It may well be true that Lester and Martin both had personal reasons for acting as they did. Lester wished to advance his claim to the Liberal candidacy for the district, at the same time discrediting Farrar—whom he regarded as his main opponent

—and solidifying his support amongst the Pentecostal congregation. Martin, perhaps, was seeking revenge for Eaton's treatment of his father. The behaviour of both underlines the opposing communities of interest which compose the competing groups, and demonstrates yet further the contrasting attitudes of the groups to change: the People's Group, this time, persistently opposing change and seeking to perpetuate the structure which had sustained them in the past, and which could continue to sustain them; the Sophisticates pursuing a vision of modernity, rejecting totally the structures and political sensibilities of the traditional leadership and themselves seeking to identify new values and constituencies of support.

In fact, the People's Group, again having the advantage of cultural affinity, derived the political advantage from these encounters. Lester solidified his support among the Pentecostalists and, as a result, was finally successful as a candidate for council. The Pentecostalists themselves became rather more active politically, putting up a number of their own adherents as candidates for council (including the Principal of their elementary school) and manning the Action-for-Joey Committee to which the adherents gave monolithic support.[8]

Case 3. THE GROUPS, AND ECONOMIC DEVELOPMENT

The third area of policy on which I wish to draw is that of economic development. The nature of the development programme pursued by the Smallwood government is well documented in the literature (see, for example, A. Perlin, 1959; Royal Commission on Economic State and Prospects of Newfoundland, 1968; Gwyn, 1968; Wadel, 1969; Thoms, 1969; Perlin, 1972; Brox, 1972; Herrick, 1968). The chaos of the rapidly spawning and equally rapidly expiring industries and the callousness of the resettlement programme (see Iverson and Matthews, 1968; Matthews, 1970) aside, Smallwood's strategy may be seen as a desperate attempt to sustain a population aware of its deprivation and aspiring to the mythical luxury of its North American neighbours. He advocated and defended industrialisation, not as a good in itself, but as the only means of Newfoundland's survival:

If I would have sleepless nights it would be because of the desperate danger of the people just flocking out of Newfoundland from their feeling that there was no future here, no future for young men, no chance of an exciting and a good life. Because of my fear of that, I went after these industries . . .[9]

But Smallwood also sought to legitimate his policy by showing it to be consistent with precedent governmental behaviour, and in so doing can be seen to have been culture-extending:

... there is only one possible policy for Newfoundland, and it is my policy.
It is my policy for only twenty years past. It was the policy of Sir Richard Squires and Sir Robert Bond and Sir William Whiteway[10] ... So I did not originate the policy ...[11]

The People's Group activists in Focaltown were content to accept the government's financial cavorting and, if questioned on policy, would produce answers that had the inimitable stamp of Smallwood over them. But their own characteristic economic stance is one of passitivity. Whilst all of the members of the People's Group and the Sophisticates' Group are businessmen, it is, as I have suggested, only among the Sophisticates that one finds any significant degree of entrepreneurial activity. Unlike his opposite number, the leader of the People's Group—Arthur Martin— has only expanded and diversified the retail aspect of his business. and then only under prompting from his brother James. His reluctance to invest in resource development or manufacturing seems to be typical of the traditional approach of the Newfoundland businessman, whose preference has always been for commerce rather than for industry and who, characteristically, has preferred to invest his capital outside Newfoundland.[12] Wayne Eaton, on the other hand, is, as we have seen, an active entrepreneur involved in the extraction and refining of resources as well as in secondary industry and commerce. But the difference extends beyond that, and is reflected in the groups' community activities.

Traditionally the outport population has sought to alleviate its immediate economic hardship by looking to the government for short-term aid, often dispensed in the form of patronage (cf. Feltham, 1959, 4). The Newfoundland coastline abounds with government-financed wharfs which have served no function other than to provide men with a few months' employment in their construction, before they realised that their only hope of salvation lay in moving to another community. Further, the patronage was unproductive: it simply reinforced the dependence of the population on such beneficence and conditioned them to seek it. It is precisely this situation that would-be brokers like Lester have sought to exploit. Their aspirations have made it imperative for them to attempt to maintain the general quiescence, mechanistic solidarity, and reluctance to organise co-operatively, of the outport population. For once that population became politically self-sufficient, the broker would be superfluous. For whatever reason, the Smallwood government gave little consideration to the development of small-scale localised resources and intermediate technology of the kind which might have provided some stability in the economy and reduced to some extent the dependence of the work force on an insecure employment market (see Freeman, 1969).

If the sustenance of the work force is contingent on the ever declining beds of copper and timber stands exploited locally, then so, to some extent, is that of the Focaltown businessman. Another mine closure could seriously damage the Focaltown economy. On the other hand, a strengthening of the hinterland economy would be of enormous benefit to Focaltown merchants: it would stabilise and perhaps even expand their market. Realising this, the Sophisticates' involvement in the politics of local economic development matches their efforts in education—and the two, of course, are not unrelated. In 1966 they formed the Chamber of Commerce which has actively sought facilities—such as an airstrip, shipping services, improved roads—which would strengthen the town as a business centre. As table 1 (p. 56) indicates, all four of the Sophisticates have held office in the Chamber of Commerce. Early in 1969, anticipating the closure of one of the three local mines, they suggested to the Focaltown town council that it call a meeting of interested local parties with a view to establishing an economic development association. The meeting was held, the Association founded, and the Sophisticates occupied two of the four executive offices—Wayne Eaton and John Whiteway as president and vice-president respectively—the two others going to a member of the Legitimisers' Group (see chapter 2, n. 10) and a non-aligned peripheral activist. Donald Farrar drafted the Association's constitution. None of the People's Group activists sought office and, indeed, only one attended the meeting at which the elections were held.

Just as Stan Lester's approach to local economic development would appear to be determined by his political ambitions, so is Eaton's influenced by personal financial considerations. At the time he became President of the Association, three of his businesses were in some difficulty. The logging enterprise could only remain profitable if he could negotiate a new contract with one of the paper companies, and increased mechanisation was making part of his work force redundant. He admitted that he had an instrumental interest in the Association: it might provide new opportunities for himself and, indeed, for the men he might lay off. He also recognised that the efficacy of the Association in the local outports might be limited through suspicion of his economic self-interest. Indeed at outport meetings of the Association, both he and John Whiteway were frequently met by such accusations. Shortly afterwards Eaton resigned the presidency and announced his intention to seek, *through the Association*, a timber concession from the government for the linerboard and chip mill he was planning to build. The mill was to cost $2½ million and involved a contracting agreement with one of the paper companies. Quite apart from his instrumental use of the Association, it is indicative of Eaton's style that he had attempted to arrange finance for the project without making any recourse—almost inevitable in Newfoundland—to the provincial government.

The Association had also, in its first four months of existence, arranged for a fishery survey, persuaded Job Brothers of St John's to establish a local fish purchasing depot, and succeeded in having another nearby community designated as a resettlement centre. Following Eaton's resignation Donald Farrar became the Association's president.

The formation of this Association by the Sophisticates, and its subsequent structure and performance, provides a model example of both their innovative tendencies and their willful deviation from traditional political values. The successful operation of such an association in the Focaltown area would be fraught with difficulties posed by local custom, regardless of the personalities involved. There is no tradition of community co-operation (cf. DeWitt, 1969, 51)—indeed, little conception of the community other than in terms of the services it provides. Traditionally there is little inclination to organise, except in pursuit of very immediate economic gain. Perhaps of most manifest difficulty is the local suspicion of Focaltowners as being self-seeking. All of these would seem to call for a more subtle introduction of the idea of regional and para-co-operative development than by an association whose executives are leading businessmen and professionals (see Dore, 1971, *passim*), especially since organisation-based assertiveness is construed locally as a challenge to established and legitimate sources of authority. The Sophisticates' advocacy of and active participation in the Association thus provides yet further demonstration of their disregard of the customary political idiom.

The issue also emphasises the contrast between the opposing groups in respect of their dichotomous orientations to and interests in change. Whilst the People's Group activists have sought to create indispensability for themselves by attempting to maintain the political *status quo*, the Sophisticates sought their own kinds of advantages in rejecting it. The members of the People's Group advocate only those kinds of development which would not threaten the traditional dependence of the outport population on the government and, secondarily, on themselves as brokers. The possibility of greater economic self-sufficiency at the local level represents a threat to the bases of their leadership just as, indeed, it would have threatened Smallwood's dominion. The Sophisticates, on the other hand, advocate forms of change demanding both new leadership structures and the entrepreneurial and organisational skills which they have developed.

It will be noticed that in each of the three cases discussed in this chapter the activity associated with the opposing attitudes of both groups is restricted to the elite group members and to their peripheral activists. The nature of both groups' activity discourages mass participation (cf. Evans' n.d., 8), except where it is demanded by an electoral campaign. The People's Group activists' portrayal of themselves as effective brokers between local communities and the provincial government has the effect of reinforcing the traditional political characteristic of dependence on a beneficent source of paternalistic authority[13] by discouraging, and making unnecessary, organisation at a grass-roots level to seek local improvements and development. The Sophisticates, on the other hand, work through organisations whose conditions of membership are strictly defined and are, therefore, exclusive (cf. DeWitt, 1969, 53), whose values are culturally alien, and whose benefits flow to a narrowly limited number of recipients. Thus, the particular situation of leadership conflict with which we are dealing tends to keep the local citizen politically quiescent, deterring the redistribution of resources between leaders and followers, and thereby frustrating vertical *political* change (cf. Banfield, 1958, 7), in the sense of the paradigm presented earlier.

The limitation of change to the level of leadership may thus be seen to be enshrined within the political objectives of each groups' activities, concerned as they are with the legitimation of their respective stances, and with their struggle to legitimate themselves as the rightful leaders in the community's changed social circumstances.

NOTES TO CHAPTER FOUR

[1] Again, I distinguish these from *brokers* proper, who performed the valuable function of purveying information for Smallwood.

[2] See, for example, the list of putative supporters of Smallwood for the Liberal Leadership in *The Loyal Liberal*, St John's, Newfoundland, 3 September 1969. A survey of such 'key men', undertaken with George Perlin, shows that leading provincial politicians use their 'key men' in widely differing ways, some possessing a great many informants, others relying on very few. One party leader named as many as fifty-seven people as his local informants, and said that he did not even know whether all of these gave him electoral support.

[3] Two industrialists of doubtful repute, to whom Smallwood gave enormous incentives and financial aid. Much of the opposition's attack on Smallwood was organised around the implication of his and his ministers' complicity in the dubious operations of such industrial promoters. Such 'pocket-lining' as Smallwood was accused of whilst he was in office has traditionally been endemic in the Newfoundland governmental system (see Noel, 1971, *passim*) and more or less overt. At the time he was certainly never popularly considered to be more guilty—probably less so—than his parliamentary colleagues of both parties. Typical inducements offered to financiers during the Smallwood era were the tax-free concessions of the Crown corporation, heavily subsidised electric power, massive direct financial grants, and exclusive concessions to vast areas of natural resources.

[4] Parts of this section appear in Cohen (1975*b*).

[5] On the development of Newfoundland's educational system see Rowe (1952).

[6] *Historical Statistics of Newfoundland and Labrador*, St John's, Government of Newfoundland and Labrador (1970). p. 10.

[7] The stigmatic nature of Pentecostalist identity in Focaltown, and the strategies employed to cope with it, are described in detail in Cohen (1975*a*).

[8] It is worth nothing that, with its heavy concentration of Pentecostalists, Herring Bay was one of only nine (out of a total of forty-two) provincial ridings which the Liberals managed to retain in the 1972 general election.

[9] *The Western Star*, Cornerbrook, Newfoundland, 26 March 1969.

[10] Previous premiers of the Dominion of Newfoundland.

[11] Quoted in Thoms (1969, 19).

[12] Dr David Alexander (personal communication, 1969) argues that but for this tradition of exporting capital, Newfoundland might have been a viable economic unit and thus would not have had to seek entry into the Canadian Confederation.

[13] Notwithstanding his populist rhetoric, Smallwood's governmental style shows many characteristics of political paternalism.

CHAPTER FIVE

Styles of articulation as strategies of myth management

In this chapter I attempt to show how the contrast between the myth-managing strategies of cultural extension and cultural substitution becomes manifest in the characteristic modes through which the groups articulate with other actors and with other levels of social action. Here again, implicit in their respective styles are the groups' claims for legitimacy in the context of a changing socio-cultural environment. The People's Group activists play new roles which they attempt to assimilate to the structures and values which informed traditional political process. The Sophisticates play more explicitly 'new' roles, and emphasise their departure from customary political practice. In the Focaltown milieu, cultural extension prescribes personal dealings, so far as possible through primary relations. Cultural substitution, on the other hand, is reflected in the secondary, organisational encounters utilised by the Sophisticates in their typical mode of articulation.

I have remarked already on the phenomenon of 'legitimacy by association' or 'extension', in which legitimacy is extended between 'persons' and 'roles'. In this regard, I noted that skilled politicians such as Premier Smallwood and Thomas Rodgers frequently used their personal legitimacy to mobilise support for some structural innovation or topical issue. That they were able to do so with such effect and frequency is both an indication and a reinforcement of the personal nature of political appeal in Newfoundland. Politicians are talked of as familiar acquaintances, and as being accessible to their constituents, for both of which there is much justification.[1] With this personalism goes the tendency to attribute salience to the political actor rather than to his official role.

There is, then, a popular impression of closeness to the leader, tempered by deference, an impression which has undoubtedly been reinforced by the legendary approachability of Joey Smallwood:

At his office, or in his home, federal ministers or corporate vice-presidents still found themselves upstaged in mid-interview by a fisherman determinedly demanding instant action on a job, a misplaced pension, or an unemployment insurance claim [Gwyn, 1968, 233–4]

To those who are set apart, either by status or by intellect, it is, as I have said, an intimacy tempered by deference. But the impression of intimacy remains, so long as the politician projects a personality which transcends his office. Possibly as a consequence, the patronising merchant, however far removed by social distance, will also earn the deference, respect, and even, perhaps, affection of his 'subjects', so long as he approaches them *as an individual* (cf. Faris, 1972, 119 ff.). But the political entrepreneur, delighting in the paraphernalia of organisation, even though he may have risen from fisherman or logger, will be treated warily, with suspicion, with an unfriendly deference, and with a lack of trust. 'Cleverness' is not an image the aspiring politician in Herring Bay should seek; impersonality is a mode and an image he should eschew.

The two types are accurately reflected by the People's Group and by the leading Sophisticates. Typically, the approaches of the People's Group activists are personal and individualistic; those of the Sophisticates are impersonal, and based on organisational role. The dichotomy will be described in terms of the activists' relations both with their 'constituents' and with the government. First, however, it is interesting to note that these stylistic differences characterise even communication *within* the groups. The People's Group members talk to each other as possessors of individual, personal experience, whilst Sophisticate deliberations are conducted more on the basis of collective—or at least shared—organisational experience. As a consequence, there is less ideological homogeneity in the first group than in the second, as one would expect given their respective attitudes to change in the structures of community leadership. The members of the People's Group are concerned with the protection of their existing and customary positions; the Sophisticates seek to undermine those positions by replacing the values which sustain them by the 'new' ethics of organisation and middle-class activism. Differences among the Sophisticates tend to be ones of degree rather than of kind. Disputes in the People's Group may be quite sharp and open. In the last municipal election both Lester and Arthur Martin were candidates. Lester's platform called for an extension of water, sewerage, and street lighting facilities; a second street through the town; paved side-roads, extended sidewalks; 'more and better recreation facilities ...' and so on. To which Arthur Martin replied in his manifesto:

> It is obvious that our town needs extended sidewalks, paved side-roads, and improved water system, a second street, more and better recreation facilities, etc. etc. but let us be very frank and honest about all this ... there is no secret or magic formula that I know of whereby we can improve our services and facilities without paying the bill ... [we] have periods when we must stop to take stock and consolidate our position. We are presently in such a period.

Even with thirteen other candidates in the field, the similarity of content leaves no doubt as to the identity of the intended target. The Sophisticates, on the other hand, seem to differ primarily in their estimation of how instrumental each should be. For example, Wayne Eaton said,

I recall trying to persuade Ivan Lush to play a more active part in the Chamber [of Commerce.] He said, 'Why? The Chamber can't do anything for me.'

and he alternates between calling his co-activists 'stalwarts' and complaining that he receives insufficient help from Ivan Lush and John Whiteway, as well as from the peripheral activists, in managing the organisations and 'promoting the town'.

There are other distinguishing characteristics of intra-group and micro-political behaviour as well. The People's Group strategies are designed to fit the personal roles of its members. Stan Lester says,

Over the last year, the stands that I have taken and what I have put into this has been purely my own—not representing any body . . .

The Sophisticates' characteristic procedure, on the other hand, is to place their strategies within an organisational context: they formulate policy as a group and then seek to implement it through the framework of an existing appropriate organisation, or through an *ad hoc* organisation which they create. As one of them relates,

I suppose informally you find the channel: you usually find an . . . existing organisation which can either handle the problem or can at least act on it to the point of discussing it openly and finding out what organisation it properly belongs to.

The stylistic differences are, of course, demonstrated even more clearly by the groups' 'macro-political' relations and the ways in which they articulate with higher and lower levels of the political scale. Figure 1 shows a diagrammatic representation of their characteristic modes of articulation.

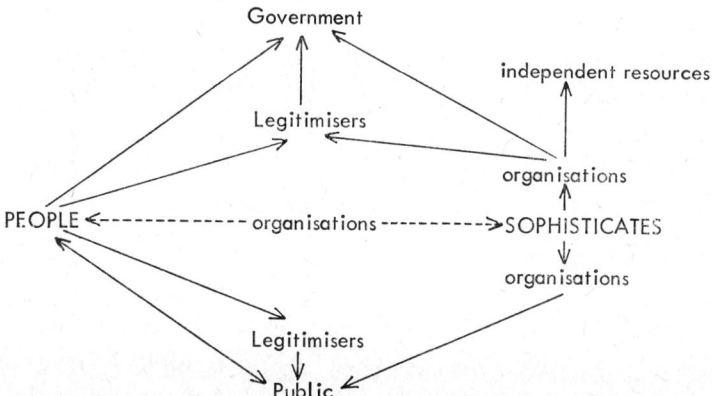

Figure 1. Modes of group articulation

78 The management of myths

By virtue of their conformity to traditional political values, the People's Group activists have 'reciprocal' communication with the public or mass, and their strategies require an active public response, whether in the forms of clientship or votes. But they do not all have the same audience. Lester directs most of his attention to communities outside Focaltown, whereas Arthur Martin does not. Even within Focaltown, it is clear that each communicates more effectively with different audiences. Lester draws most of his support from the Pentecostalists in the low-income east end of town; Martin is strongest in the central and west sections of town, the centre containing the old-established Methodist and Anglican families, and the west end containing a new subdivision housing the mining company's executives and many of the more affluent Focaltowners. A small shanty section in the west end is being gradually depopulated by migration to the east. Table 2 is a breakdown of the town by polling district, showing the proportion of votes received in each district by Lester, Martin and Lush, in the municipal election of 1969, and showing the predominant features of the districts' electorates. Districts 1 and 2 are the west and central sections respectively; district 3—the margin between the central and east sections—is the fringe of the Pentecostalist area and is also heavily Salvationist; and district 4—the 'east end'—is where the Pentecostalists are most densely concentrated. It may be seen that Lester's strength, relative to Martin's, is greatest in districts 3 and 4 (indeed, is almost equal to it in the latter), is less in district 2, and weakest in district 1. Note also that the Sophisticate candidate, Ivan Lush, polls heaviest in district 1 (the high income section), much less well in district 2 where Martin actually tops the poll, and poorly in the low income and Pentecostalist districts.

Table 2. Positions in poll, percentages of votes, and predominant electoral features, by polling district: Focaltown municipal election, November 1969

	Lester		Martin		Lush	
	Position	%	Position	%	Position	%
Overall	7	7·62	2	10·68	4	8·49
District 1 'West end'; new subdivision; executive and affluents	9	6·27	3	10·19	2	10·34
District 2 Town centre; old-established families, Methodists and Anglicans	6	8·05	1	11·5	5	8·57
District 3 Pentecostalist fringe; Salvationists	5	8·06	2	10·97	8	6·56
District 4 'East end'; Pentecostalist concentration	5	9·09	3	9·28	7	7·16

Note: Each elector may vote for up to seven candidates. This explains the small percentage of the total ward vote that any candidate is able to achieve.

We saw earlier that Stan Lester assumes the role of broker for some of the smaller local communities in their relations with the government. As I have suggested previously, his brokerage or mediation is present only in his clients' approaches to the patron, not the reverse. I have suggested, also, that his role in this respect is self-appointed, and is being used as a springboard to formal leadership office. It is, indeed, questionable whether he is actually a broker at all. Here, I have to digress from Focaltown politics to clarify my reservations about allowing Lester the title of broker.[2]

The politics of legitimacy in Focaltown may be seen to consist largely in the competitive attempts made by opposed groups of activists to manage the meanings which the local people perceive in their leadership behaviour and, more generally, in the political milieu. Politicians, like all social actors who engage in strategic presentation, seek to contrive particular interpretations of their behaviour and of the contexts within which they perform. The broker is, *par excellence*, such an actor.

The nature of the broker role has received extensive discussion in the literature, much of it concerned to make taxonomic distinctions both between the broker and the patron, and between the broker and other 'intermediary' roles (see, for example, Boissevain, 1966; 1974; Foster, 1963; Mayer, 1967; Paine, 1971; Silverman, 1965; Wolf, 1966). In this latter regard, Paine suggests that the broker be distinguished from other intermediary roles by his peculiar activity of mediating or 'processing' information with the intention of changing its emphasis and or content (*op. cit.*, 21; 1973, 27 ff. Also see Bailey, 1969, 167 ff.). This would seem to tap a crucial and diacritical dimension of brokerage, and suggests a logic which needs to be developed a little further to arrive at the distinctive political capabilities of the broker. Students of politics have generally seen the broker's function to be the bringing together of a patron and clients in response to *their* mutual needs. One might argue though that, as a manager of meaning, the broker may actually provoke those needs himself. He may create a demand for values among potential clients, persuade a 'patron' that he, indeed, has resources of patronage to dispense and of the desirability of having clients obligated to him. In so doing, he creates a demand for his services among both patron and clients.[3] The broker role is not, then, called into being simply by the desire of two parties to transact valued items: rather, it creates, or may create the demand for those values in the interacting parties. In so doing, it seeks (through the management of meaning) to contrive indispensability for itself, and it is on the perception of his indispensability by both patron and client that the broker's success rests.

It may be objected that political interaction breeds few indispensabilities. However, strategic presentational behaviour is essentially exaggerated behaviour and, as such, frequently translates the long-term expediency into the short-term necessity. The mere 'usefulness' which the observer perceives in the intermediary may, in the exigency of the moment, seem *crucial* to one or both of the parties between whom he mediates. The quintessential political career is the one built upon the contrivance and exploitation of such situations. But politics is littered with unsuccessful attempts. Societies which have, like Newfoundland, traditionally articulated centre and periphery through patronage are full of men who have sought such indispensability and have failed. The broker who becomes dispensable ceases to be a 'broker' in any meaningful political sense.

Lester has never achieved such indispensability. He has been used as a middleman both by clients (outports) and patron (Smallwood), and I have called attention to the difficulties involved in making the phenomenological distinction between expediency and necessity in the political short term. However, his participation in relations between patron and client seems always to have been determined by *their* choice, rather than by his success in creating a need for his services. Lester's entire political strategy is directed towards obscuring his essential dispensability (see Cohen and Comaroff, 1975). He presents himself to his 'clients' not as simply a successful broker but as one who satisfies the customary criteria of legitimate political brokerage. Further, he presents them with an interpretation of their relations with the patron which fits it in to—renders it intelligible within—their experience of political behaviour. In the course of this strategic presentation of self, Lester does engage in the kind of behaviour which is associated with brokerage. He does purvey a valued commodity to the patron—he delivers the votes—and he does 'process' information by selective communication to clients concerning resources available from the government. In this respect he creates expectations which he then seeks to satisfy, and to be seen to satisfy, through his relations with the patron, in order to further his political career. As I have mentioned, he also sets out to manage meanings in ways which may be typically identified with the broker. Firstly, he attempts to contrive meanings for the interaction between client and patron which create a role for himself, and make that role intelligible within the terms of his clients' cultural experience. Secondly, he seeks to contrive a meaning for the nature of his own behaviour as broker, which is tantamount to legitimation.

But despite his attempts to make himself into a broker, Lester does not display the distinctive characteristic of indispensability. To the client outports in Herring Bay he is more important as a 'foolish leader'—a scapegoat—than as a vital procurer of services. He has no power with respect to the patron by whom he is, rather, tolerated. For reasons I have mentioned earlier (chapter 3) it was politic for Smallwood to maintain local men in the guise of brokers. But it was by Smallwood's choice that they were allowed such guises, and at his whim that they were used. The distinctive feature of Smallwood patronage in Herring Bay was that the 'broker' was employed in the prestation of client to patron, but not the reverse, for that would have diluted the value—Smallwood's ability to monopolise political support and control local careers. Only the premier could be seen to have the ability to dispense valued items. Lester was not indispensable to the patron, for there were always other ambitious men who could be called upon.

There are, then, respects in which Lester approximates the broker model, and others in which he does not. There are aspects of his performance which may produce in at least a minority of his clients the belief that he does possess the attributes of indispensability, although this is not generally the case. But of greatest importance is that Lester *perceives himself* to possess the attributes of broker set out in the model, and plans his role strategy accordingly. It is for this reason that I call him a 'would-be broker'. I now return to the case material.

I have suggested, then, that in making personal, individualistic approaches to these outlying communities, Lester attempts to manipulate their aspirations and create expectations. One example involves a small community some thirty miles from Focaltown, which had previously been the property of a mining company. When the copper was exhausted, the company moved out, leaving behind such facilities as water and sewerage systems, fire fighting equipment, street lighting, a community hall, a community TV antenna, and so on. The community—Company Cove—could not make use of these facilities since it was not a corporate body and, therefore, there was no one to whom the company could legally hand them over. Stan Lester went into Company Cove with a twofold objective. Firstly, he sought to ingratiate himself with the community by showing its citizens how they could acquire the facilities: they must petition, under his guidance, for municipal status. Having achieved that, the Company would sign over its property for one dollar. He thus sought to create a demand, help to satisfy it, and reap the benefit in the form of electoral support in his pursuit of the Liberal candidacy. Secondly, he sought to ingratiate himself with the government by persuading two settlements nearby to resettle in Company Cove:

I told Mr Rowe, the Deputy Minister of Municipal Affairs, that there was a good chance of centralising a group of people there because the way I look at this is: it is a sin to have a place such as Company Cove, with a six-room school there for which you could get the services of fairly qualified teachers, whereas various places like Fudge's Arm and Point Harbour, which I visit, have one- and two-room schools, which is not adequate any more. I felt that if we could get these people to eventually see what is happening there in Company Cove, they'd say, 'Well, you know, we can't stay here; we don't have any water or any sewage and the services are practically nil . . . '

Success would bring him not only the gratitude of the people of Fudge's Arm and Point Harbour for showing them the way to the material conveniences of North American life, but also the gratitude of the government for eliminating two more communities and thus enhance the likelihood of it supporting his claim for the Liberal nomination. His motives, then, can be regarded, with some justification, as being those of political self-interest; his characteristic mode of articulation is individualistic.

His approaches to the government are also made on a personal and individualistic basis. He exploits the informality of Newfoundland politics, and spurns the organisation as a medium of articulation. In so doing, he is not merely exercising his ego: he is also being pragmatic, and making an important comment on the nature of traditional political communication:

Here in Focaltown we have been fortunate, in a sense, in that over the years we have had people like Mayor Rodgers ... He was a very close friend of the premier and if you are trying to do anything for the community, if you don't have any close contact with the people concerned—Ministers and so on—you can't do anything ...

Arthur Martin agreed, suggesting that the most important resource of the successful politician is

... not what you know—it's who you know. You need the proper contacts, you can't do it alone ... You've got to have connections to the right contacts ... you got to have the co-operation of the right people in the right places ...

Indeed, Lester attributes his influence in those communities in which he has sought to establish himself as a broker to the fact that the local population misconceives the nature of the government and fails to recognise both the feasibility and the efficacy of making personal approaches themselves:

They don't really know what the government is and they look at government as some big organisation that is far from their reach ...

In fact, this raises one of the many paradoxes which help to explain the personal salience of politicians in Newfoundland. For while the government, as an institutional galaxy, is seen as a remote, omnipotent, and vaguely sinister bureaucratic monolith, the leader—'Joey'— is felt to be within almost universal reach, and this image of accessability extends to many politicians: as I mentioned at the beginning of this chapter, a politician acquires support as his personality or image transcends his office. By the same token, the longevity of the Smallwood administration was not evidence of any deep-rooted Liberalism so much as it signified a political movement rooted in the tradition and culture of Newfoundland and *personified* in Smallwood. Just as the perceptual distinction is made between the institution of the government and its members, so was one made between the Liberal Party and Smallwood: in a sample of 391 respondents, 47 per cent of those who could name four leading members of the provincial Liberal Party did *not* name Smallwood—he is regarded as 'above' or 'apart from' the Party. The man is salient; the institutional base is not. But even whilst the politician is felt to be accessible and can easily be identified with, his constituents exhibit an uneasy feeling of their own inadequacy—almost unworthiness—which leads them to seek a representative or a spokesman (cf. Stiles, 1971). Formal leadership roles can be easily monopolised in the Newfoundland outport, for the general reluctance to assume them is so widespread. It is on this reticence that men such as Stan Lester seek to build their ascendancy.

So far, then, we have noted two main themes in Lester's articulation with the government. Firstly, he believes in the efficacy of the personal approach. Secondly, he believes in the necessity of maintaining close personal relations with members of the government. Not surprisingly, there is a third: he believes devoutly both in his personal efficacy and in the intimacy of his own relationships with the government:

I have been very closely connected with the premier and his Cabinet for the past several years and I am privileged, in a sense, to be able to go into St John's and in the Confederation [government] Building, and without any appointment or anything, I can pretty well see any of these fellows at any time.

And again,

I am not saying that this is the way it should be but I am saying that this is the way it has been and always will be. Any member of the government is either a friend of yours or he is not. If he's not you don't expect to get the same results— if you do, you're crazy. As I have said, I can go to the Confederation Building today and I venture to say that by 6 o'clock this evening I could see every department head that is in there . . .

Clearly, then, he attaches most salience to direct and personal communication.

But, as Figure 1 suggests, there is another channel of communication which the People's Group, like the Sophisticates, occasionally uses, provided by a third group of activists—the Legitimisers. These are activists whose *institutional roles* may—as the name suggests—lend legitimacy to the activities of whichever group happens to seek it. Typically, the Legitimisers occupy official leadership roles in the culturally sanctioned institutions which are perceived to be neutral in, or unrelated to, most of the partisan conflicts which inform community life. As a consequence, the Legitimisers are perceived as being 'non-political' leaders—men with no 'personal' stake in their positions of authority. They are generally outsiders who, unlike the Sophisticates, can exercise 'legitimate' leadership by virtue *of their institutional roles*. The fact that they *are* outsiders, and that they do not have to create their own leadership positions, helps to account for their neutrality. There were three main activists in this category whilst the study was being made (one has since left Focaltown). Firstly, there was the senior doctor at the local hospital, who came to Focaltown from Britain in the late 1950s. He succeeded Thomas Rodgers in the mayoralty, and following the 1969 municipal election was deputy mayor. He was also secretary-treasurer of the Focaltown branch of the Canadian Legion, and was peripherally involved in the Liberal Party—simply, he says, in order to have a position from which he could bargain with the (Liberal) government for improvements to the hospital. Indeed, he attributes the eventual success of his request for a $300,000 extension to the hospital partly to his position as a (highly influential) delegate to the 1969 Liberal leadership convention—at which he gratefully supported Mr Smallwood. He is self-consciously neutral in his public dealings, but is inclined to sympathise privately with the People's Group activists, particularly with Thomas Rodgers and Arthur Martin:

There is a certain amount of competition but I just keep out of it, I just keep neutral. I refuse to discuss it—this is the best way to go about it.

A second Legitimiser is the magistrate who, in Newfoundland outports, is a resident stipendiary official. The office itself has great legitimacy. Prior to Confederation the magistrate was often the only representative of the distant St John's government. In the present magistrate's words,

A magistrate under Commission government was the be all and end all. He was the senior civil servant . . . the Minister of Justice referred to us as having the most prestigious job in the Province of Newfoundland and I think this dates from the time when the magistrates had . . . powers over everything—health facilities, calling an election, forming a co-operative, even setting up water and sewerage systems.

The incumbent was accorded the kind of respectful deference that might be more familiarly reserved for the squirearchy.[4]

The Focaltown magistrate during the period covered in this study was somewhat unlikely as an object of deference and, indeed, discouraged it:

I think a great many civil servants make the mistake of wanting to be called 'Mr' or 'Sir' . . .

He is, nevertheless, held in great regard locally, a tribute, perhaps, to his skilful impression management. A celebrated raconteur—a much valued attribute in Newfoundland (cf. Faris, 1972)—he proudly boasts the crudest tongue in Herring Bay. He is very active in the Lions Club, Chairman of the Red Cross Committee, Chairman of the Stadium Commission, and a campaigner for a host of issues. His first organisational love, though, is the Lions Club and his activity in it is, unlike that of the Sophisticates' activists, regarded as being totally altruistic:

... we feel that we owe the community something and that it is our responsibility to give this community the best that we have.

The third Legitimiser was the personnel officer for one of the local mining companies. His standing in the community was such as to be recognised in his being dubbed 'Uncle' (see chapter 3, note 8). He was the secretary-treasurer of the Legion, and of the Chamber of Commerce, a town councillor, a member of the Library Board, past president of the Lions Club—and, because of his diligence, the almost inevitable choice for the most burdensome office in any organisation. He fits almost exactly the model which F. J. Evans notes as a ubiquitous Newfoundland phenomenon and calls 'the foolish leader' (personal communication): a person, frequently an outsider, thrust into a position of responsibility who will be made to take the blame for things that go wrong, but will be denied the credit, for those that 'go right'. He approximates the scapegoated stranger observed in a Welsh village by Frankenberg (1957, 98, 131). His role was that of executive rather than policy-maker: he was excluded, both by inclination and by Sophisticate design, from decision-making.

In addition to these three there are a number of peripheral activists who become Legitimisers by virtue of their assumption of particular roles, and these would include the remaining non-aligned councillors.

The principal Legitimisers therefore have in common that they are outsiders who have come to Focaltown as employees of external agencies (the Departments of Health and Justice, and the mining companies), and who, therefore, have no personal financial stake in social and economic process in Focaltown. Secondly, their occupations—senior doctor, magistrate, personnel manager—put them in authoritative positions *vis-à-vis* substantial numbers of the community's population. Thirdly, they all perform culturally legitimate political and administrative roles. Finally, they exhibit neutrality in Focaltown politics.

Figure 1 shows that both the People's Group and the Sophisticates use the Legitimisers. The Sophisticates would seem to stand in greater need since their roles overlap with typically legitimate ones to a much lesser extent than do those of the People's Group: all three of the latter are, or have been councillors, two as mayor. Of the Sophisticates, one is an ex-councillor, and one currently serves on council—although his known ambition *and* association with Sophisticate organisations tends to deny him legitimacy even in that role. The People's Group activists often act through the media of the legitimate offices of which they are themselves incumbents. In this way they garner deference in their articulation with the public, and conserve their *personal* resources and articulation with the government. But further, they attempt to impress the public by their association with the Legitimisers and, indeed, with the achievements of the Legitimisers. Thus, for example, Stan Lester says in a deliberately worded sentence of his election manifesto:

Over the past years, I have had the opportunity to work with *our former mayor*, Mr T. Rodgers, and our *present mayor*, Dr ——, especially on the day *we* received assurance from the Minister of Health and Premier Smallwood that the extension of the Focaltown Cottage Hospital would go ahead as planned. [My italics]

He also comments, suggestively, on the importance of a leader not having a financial or organisational stake in the community, thereby underlining the impartiality of the Legitimisers, and posing a sharp contrast to the Sophisticates' typical self-justifications of 'We, the taxpayers, etc.':

I think what we have to look for is . . . the person that doesn't really have too many business ties and a person that we know is going to go in there for the sole purpose of doing a good job. I'm not at all sure that a businessman is the right leader.

The People's Group activists argue the predominance of the legitimate political institutions over those typically of the Sophisticates. Quite unlike their opponents who, to a man, said the contrary, the People's Group members all named the town council as the most important and powerful organisation, and the mayor's as the most powerful institutional role, in Focaltown. While the Sophisticates were highly critical of the council, the People's Group activists laud its achievements. Thus, Arthur Martin says,

. . . this town wouldn't be nearly as advanced as it is if we had not had a town council . . . I think it's had a greater effect, a greater bearing, on the development of the town than any organisation I know.

Martin 'depersonalises' himself in Focaltown, to emphasise his legitimate institutional role. In his election manifesto he does not ask people to vote *for him*: he simply commends them to 'VOTE'. He comments on the fact that fifteen candidates were seeking the seven council seats—

. . . a very good indication of interest in local government affairs.

Like all the other candidates he mentioned that several people asked him to seek re-election (to admit that he had done so uninvited would imply assertiveness), but suggests that this was because of his *role* rather than because of his personal attributes:

... at least ten people felt my experience as deputy mayor over the past eight years should be helpful ...

In sum, he poses as adviser rather than as politician, as one who is lifted above the fray of cruder political mortals by both the dignity of his ascriptive attributes, the dedication of his institutional role, and his paternalistic concern for the welfare of his subjects. He is a collection of roles wedded together by altruism—but just enough of a person that the citizens remember who he is. But his rhetorical self-image is, for electoral purposes, that of the responsible public official.

The People's Group members thus insinuate themselves into an appearance of institutional legitimacy and seek to identify themselves with the three activists whose roles carry the most legitimacy—the Legitimisers. When they articulate with the government in this way, they do so, as I suggested, to conserve their personal good standing. It is notable that Lester only uses the Legitimisers in his Focaltown activities, never in his 'brokerage' functions on behalf of the outlying settlements. And even then he only uses them, first, when he will not personally lose face if he is unsuccessful, and secondly, when he *would* lose face if he did not enter the issue. The first case would obtain when several other activists were involved with him in making an input to the government. Two examples here are the campaigns waged by the Chamber of Commerce, the Lions Club, and the town council, to have the access road to the Trans-Canada Highway paved, and to obtain a government-financed extension to the hospital. Lester claims to have been instrumental in both of these campaigns, but the important point is that had the campaigns failed, he could have saved face with his local constituents by pointing to the failure of *all* the petitioners, and could, at the same time, have exonerated himself with the government by hiding among all the other participants—by pointing out not only that his was not the lone voice, but that among the collective roars of the Chamber, the Lions Club and the council it was insignificant. The second case applies precisely when all the other activists and organisations have combined to make an input. If he were to stay out, and they succeeded, he would be forced to admit their political efficacy. But if he joins, and they succeed, he can attribute the success—as he does —to his own intervention.

The final point in relation to the People's Group is that since its 'upward' articulation is oriented solely towards the government, the roles and incumbents of legitimacy offer its activists their only means of indirect communication. They do not have the Sophisticates' device of the organisation, nor their alternative recourse to independent resources.

The substantive conclusion is, thus, that the People's Group members' modes of articulation, whether they are based on the personal approach or on traditionally legitimate roles, are quite congruent with the values of the customary political culture: they are, indeed, the typical modes of articulation in the Newfoundland political tradition. In so far as they are now employed in modified structural conditions, the People's Group's behaviour may be seen, again, to be culture-extending.

Figure 1 shows that, with one exception, all of the People's Group's lines of articulation are direct and personal: even whilst they may make an indirect approach to the government through the Legitimisers, their approach to the Legitimisers is personal. The one exception is their line of articulation to the Sophisticates: it has to run through an organisation since they only 'meet' each other in organisational contexts. The diagram also shows that the Sophisticates make *no* personal approaches: their articulation with extra-governmental agencies, with the government, with the Legitimisers, and with the public, all takes place through organisations. Further, in so far as they do articulate with the public through organisations, the articulation is not reciprocated. They do not seek public participation in their cause; the public does not seek to communicate politically with the Sophisticates since their values are alien. As we have seen earlier, the very nature of the group suggests a rejection of customary values.

The Sophisticates' approaches to the public consist simply in the 'services' they provide through their organisations. Whether these are the facilities provided by the Lions Club—the ice rink, the bus shelters, the Labour Day and Winter Carnivals—or the community 'representation' and legislative decisions made by the Chamber of Commerce and, later, the Economic Development Association, the public is not consulted. The Sophisticates, or their organisations, make the decision and implement it. Their deliberate rejection of traditional values is matched by their intentional neglect of popular demands and opinion, and derives from their belief that their personal career successes are proof of their ability to set priorities for the community. As one informant said,

... the fact that they have been successful, have made some money and everything, is ... usually a pretty good indication that they can also make a contribution in other ways ... If you are successful in one area, usually you can be in other areas as well. Nothing succeeds like success, see?

But they further believe that they have the *right* to set such priorities. This is, of course, a value that they do not often make explicit. But it is implicit in the nature of the Sophisticates' manipulation of their various organisations, which I shall describe in the context of mobilisation strategies. I should emphasise here that they do not consciously express the intrinsic justice of elite predominance: they simply do not question it. One Sophisticate informant, having named his colleagues, said,

... I don't think we see ourselves consciously as any kind of power group. It's only if you sit down and think about it like this that you realise that ... the ... people I mentioned are there when there is a job to be done.

It is not a philosophy portrayed as good and set against another which is bad: it is seen simply to be self-evidently true.

They thus make unreciprocated approaches to the public and they do not seek reciprocation. Their legitimacy would be manifest not in demonstrable public support but in the tacit recognition that their organisations are effective and based on sound values and principles, and should therefore be left to get on with the business of leadership. Much of this is implicit in the philosophy of cultural substitution. But it is also, perhaps, a reaction to the personal difficulties the Sophisticates experience which follow from their cultural 'distance' from the local people. They cannot conduct their relations in the local idiom of intimacy, for their motives constantly attract suspicion and they are, anyway, perceived as too distant on account of their 'modern' social careers. Their recourse to the organisational façade might also be explained, then, as an adaptation forced upon them, as well as in terms of their ideology of leadership.

Their *upward* articulation is, similarly, made impersonally through organisations, but they have an additional object of articulation not available to the People's Group. Through the organisations, they are able to collect a considerable amount of money for community projects, departing from the outport's traditional dependence on, and inclination to seek, government largesse—both conditioned by an inability to organise and by the political advantages which accrue to the government from having grateful subjects. The Lions Club alone collected $15,000 annually during the period of fieldwork. The Stadium Commission was required to raise $75,000 locally, which it did, and later added a further $55,000 to this amount. The Sophisticates' organisational activity also brings them into contact with similarly involved people in other communities and with other patrons at 'higher' levels of society.

The Sophisticates nearly always act through the institutional façades of their organisations. But their decision whether or not to employ the medium of the Legitimisers is guided mainly by pragmatic considerations. The only general principle guiding that choice seems to be, firstly, that if they are in danger of being identified as the prime movers of the action, rather than their organisations or 'collective wills', they will attempt to involve the Legitimisers; and secondly, if their involvement in an issue is likely to be perceived as being self-interested they will, again, seek to use the Legitimisers. The Sophisticates have little regard for the intelligence or organisational skills of the Legitimisers, with the exception of the magistrate. The doctor is seen as being largely incompetent in matters of leadership; the personnel officer is regarded as a dupe. I mentioned the contrast between the assessments of the town council made by the People's Group and by the Sophisticates. The Sophisticates' critical evaluation is symptomatic of their attitudes to the offices and incumbents of 'legitimate' leadership in Focaltown. For example, before the last municipal election, Wayne Eaton said:

... there should be a change [in the council] ... there are businessmen who are continuously saying in my presence, 'We've got to do something about it ... we have a lack of business management within the council.

And of the then mayor (the doctor), he said:

I suggest that the reason he was elected—and for the same reason that Arthur Martin has been elected and re-elected—is that up to that time he never had, and Arthur Martin never has, in his life stuck his neck out in the community. The individuals on council are involved in such a way that they have never been known to pick a cause and stand on it, or get up in a meeting and say, 'This is what I think and I have strong feelings on it'. Those kind of people get elected because they are considered by the people as being very good guys and they are not going to upset the *status quo*, whereas someone like myself is considered a little bit radical perhaps and dangerous to the *status quo*.

Donald Farrar expresses their attitude perfectly:

... the Lions Club ... is certainly much more of a catalyst. Well, put it this way: the town council is not a catalyst at all in this community, and I think that having this huge organisation, the Lions Club, in this community, cramps the style of the town council considerably.

And John Whiteway contents himself with,

... the present council haven't done that much. It's nothing next to the Lions Club ...

These statements underline the pragmatism of the principles governing their decisions to employ the Legitimisers as a medium of articulation. These principles may be illustrated by three instances of the Sophisticates' use of the Legitimisers, two of which occurred during the course of this study, and one which took place immediately before.

1. THE STADIUM

Some years ago the Lions Club suggested that Focaltown should have a stadium, incorporating an ice-hockey arena and a curling rink. Shortly after the Chamber of Commerce was organised it took up the issue and, in Farrar's understated phrase, 'these organisations put pressure on the town council'. A little later the government announced a special programme of financial assistance for recreational facilities, proposing also the establishment of local commissions to manage them. Again, under intensive pressure from the Chamber of Commerce, the council established a Stadium Commission and appointed a chairman. In fact, by the Sophisticates' own admission, they used both the Lions Club and the Chamber of Commerce to establish the Stadium Commission and select a chairman, and employed the town council to conceal their own instrumentality:

> When the subject of the Stadium Commission chairmanship came up, we wondered who should get it. We looked around, and the three or four people already involved [i.e. the informant's fellow Sophisticates] were fairly busy and closely identified with other projects. So we looked for somebody else and [the magistrate] was named. The four of us were appointed to the Commission and served with the Commission under the magistrate's chairmanship.

The Lions Club pledged $5,000 annually to the Stadium Fund; and Wayne Eaton resigned from the Commission to bid for the construction of the project. Note that in this instance, the Sophisticates' strategic use of the Legitimisers concealed their personal roles and their possible self-interest, both from the government and from the local population. This is true also of the second case.

2. THE ECONOMIC DEVELOPMENT ASSOCIATION

Wayne Eaton often describes the retail businesses of Focaltown as being geared to the requirements of a population at least double the size of that which it now serves. As a consequence he sees a *reduction* of the population, or of its spending power, as disturbing.[5] The town is kept in a state of insecurity by the instability of markets and prices for copper, mined locally, and by the mining companies' calculated reluctance to make public long-term predictions about the extent and feasibility of the ore deposits. One of the major companies, whose mine was located close to Focaltown, limited its prognoses to two-year periods, and as a result, there was constant speculation in Focaltown about just how long the mine would last.[6] The insecurity intensified when one of the three local mines, owned by the —— Copper Company, situated fifteen miles from Focaltown, ceased operation. We have seen already that the Sophisticates responded to this by setting up the Economic Development Association, which they subsequently controlled. I wish to draw attention firstly to the way in which they created the Association, and secondly to the manner in which it then approached the local population.

The first is simple. As a ritual of innovation, its procedure was very similar to that followed in connection with the Stadium Commission. The Chamber of Commerce, acting on the initiative and proposals of the Sophisticates, wrote to the town council suggesting that it should call a meeting of the other councils in the area to discuss the economic situation. The council, of course, agreed, seeing the proposal as innocuous. But once the meeting was convened, the Sophisticates took over. Wayne Eaton spoke at length on the need to stimulate further economic growth in the area and proposed that a Development Association be formed, embracing Herring Bay:

I said ... that I was interested as a businessman in being a party to it because I owe my living to this community and the area ... and I don't think that we can take out of the community without putting something back ...

He was elected president, and an Interim Planning Committee was formed, composed of himself, Donald Farrar as secretary, James Martin (the non-aligned brother of Arthur and Frank), who was then President of the Chamber of Commerce, and a peripheral activist of the Legitimisers' Group. The committee met twice and, under its guise, Farrar and Eaton produced a constitution for the Association, proposing a structure based on district zones, each of which would be represented on the executive. They then called a further meeting, to which they invited the founding members of the Association, *representatives* of all the local councils and unincorporated communities, and *all* of the members of the Focaltown Chamber of Commerce, '... which originated the idea of this Association'.

The intention, it would seem, was, firstly, to demonstrate that Focaltown, and particularly its merchants, had the greatest stake in the economic health of the area; and secondly, to attempt to ensure the election to the executive of the Sophisticate candidates. Eaton had already been elected president. Each of the other three Sophisticates sought one of the remaining executive offices: John Whiteway successfully contested the vice-presidency; Donald Farrar and Ivan Lush stood for the posts of secretary and treasurer respectively, and lost. Their defeats did not, however, interfere with the Sophisticates' control of decision-making, and were not unexpected. Indeed, their control was enhanced, for the successful candidates served to obscure the other Sophisticates' covert involvement. The secretary was the same peripheral Legitimiser who had served on the interim committee, and was easily manipulable; the treasurer was a local teacher whose commitment was to the development of a local fishing industry with which the Sophisticates anyway sympathised. Both came from small communities outside Focaltown and this, itself, was useful in so far as it diluted the appearance of Focaltown (Sophisticate) control. Later, as I have said, Eaton resigned the presidency and was succeeded by Donald Farrar, who centralised the decision-making powers of the Association to an even greater extent.

Thus, in typical fashion, they conceived an idea, then sought to endow it with legitimacy through the offices of the council and extraneous Legitimisers, and then retrieved it to be moulded into its desired shape.

Having thus created the organisation, they tried to approach the public through it, rather than in person, hoping that sufficient legitimacy would have rubbed off onto its offices to obscure their incumbency of them. Once the organisation was established in Herring Bay, with the zone committees constituted and functioning, they would not need to approach the public at all, but would communicate simply with the representatives on the zone committees. Their suffering, then, would end with the formation and organisation of the zone committees. And they did suffer. Wayne Eaton admitted that he felt his presence as president at organisational meetings round the Bay distracted the audience from recognising the potential utility of the Association:

They see me, Wayne Eaton, a Focaltown businessman, and they think, 'Well, that guy wants to get his hands in our pockets. We're not going to help him' ... or they see a fellow like Donald [Farrar]: they won't tackle him because they know he can put them down with one remark.

Even John Whiteway who, because of his years as a Ranger in the district, is one of the better known and respected men in Focaltown, encountered suspicion of his motives:

You know, I could see them thinking, 'Well, he must be in it for something—what's he getting out of it? He's an outsider and he's a businessman.' They weren't going to help us—no Sir! They didn't see we was trying to help them.

Eventually, Eaton decided to appoint a field officer who would present a front of impartiality.[7] The position was originally intended to have both research and liaison functions, and was to be filled by a social science graduate—preferably one with knowledge of the locality. It had not been filled by the time Eaton resigned the presidency. Farrar, perhaps fearing his inability to control the work of such a person, turned it into a quasi-clerical job to which he appointed a retired magistrate, who was thought to know little or nothing about the area.

The substantive point again is that articulation with the public is impersonal and mediated by organisational structures in pursuit of an image of legitimacy, itself contingent upon a denial of self-interest. In both of these cases, the strategic ritual may be seen to have both expressive and instrumental functions. It symbolically implies the myths which underlie the use of modernistic organisational structures and which inform the ideology of middle-class entrepreneurial activism. Its instrumental purpose is to conceal, and thus to attempt to legitimate, the involvement of the Sophisticate activists. It is a means by which they hope to obscure their suspect motives behind the anonymous façade of the organisation. Both functions emphasise the Sophisticates' social and cultural distance from the great mass of the local population.

3. WAYNE EATON VS THE NEWSPAPER EDITOR

The final example is perhaps the most interesting because it is an instance of the Sophisticates' failure to conceal their involvement, and the consequent degeneration of an argument into a quite vicious public confrontation. Here, they attempt to employ the typical innovative ritual of organisational articulation, but their 'cover' is blown, and they are revealed as individual aggressors. The *Focaltown News* was a fortnightly newspaper founded and edited by the wife of the third Legitimiser, the personnel officer. In late December 1968, she was one of the subjects of a nationally-networked television programme. She had come to Focaltown six years previously from the mainland, had never particularly liked the town, and, partly, perhaps, on account of her somewhat uncompromising individuality, was not particularly liked. On the television interview, she was characteristically frank:

When I first came, this was the most God-awful place you could ever imagine.

And

... they asked, 'What do you think of Focaltown?' And I said, 'Well, I suppose it's a town like every other town. There is poverty, and a lot of people on welfare.' All of which is perfectly true.

The film portion had also shown some of the older parts of town (including an outhouse which no one was subsequently able to locate). The effect of the programme on Focaltown was cataclysmic. Some of the townspeople refused to talk to her. An open-line programme on the regional radio station was bombarded with complaints and denunciations of 'mainlanders' and 'outsiders'. And Wayne Eaton first cancelled his firm's advertising in her paper, and then set out to launch a campaign to censor her, seeking, at first, to conceal his personal involvement. He persuaded a non-aligned merchant to call a meeting of all the businessmen in the town. They convened and, having generated an atmosphere of indignation, Eaton suggested they should call a meeting of the Chamber of Commerce, to discuss what action should be taken. It was necessary that this call to the Chamber should come from a collective body, since an extraordinary meeting would have to be convened by the Chamber's secretary-treasurer, who happened to be the lady's husband. Clearly, Eaton could not have made a personal and direct request to him for such a meeting. The Chamber decided to demand a public apology from the lady, and also—the typical Sophisticate move—to request the mayor (who, at that time, was the doctor referred to earlier) to write a letter on behalf of the town council to the television network, seeking an apology from the programme's director. The lady editor, of course, contemptuously ignored the demand (having first indignantly protested that she had been prohibited from attending the Chamber's meeting in her journalistic capacity). The mayor, however, was not quite so resilient:

... the Chamber of Commerce wrote a letter to the council expressing their desire that the council should take some sort of action about this and write some comment, and I was, of course, the sucker who had to do it: I had to write the letter ... We were prompted by the Chamber of Commerce because, of course, as far as they were concerned, an affront to the town was an affront to their businesses ... that's what they were worrying about.

However, the editor's husband who, as I have pointed out, was the secretary of the Chamber of Commerce, checked the by-laws and found that the meeting had been improperly convened, was out of order, and therefore that its decisions and actions had no legality. Eaton now had three alternatives: he could pursue the matter in the Chamber of Commerce, thus getting into a fight with the Legitimisers and risking the survival of the Chamber, an organisation he had created himself; secondly, he could drop the issue altogether, but risk losing face, both among the businessmen and with the editor; and thirdly, he could pursue the matter as an individual, counting on the support of the businessmen. He decided on the latter. As it emerged, far from being supported by the businessmen (many of whom are involved with the People's Group), he found himself fighting a lone and petty battle—on his opponent's ground: the newspaper.

In the weeks following the Chamber's meeting the editor published letters of support, most of them written by friends who were the wives of her husband's company colleagues—mainlanders, like herself. But then, one of the teachers—the Principal of the amalgamated elementary school —intervened to bring the matter to a head again, ridiculing the mayor for criticising a programme he had not even seen, suggesting that the townspeople had exhibited a total absence of any sense of humour, and expressing relief at seeing

... that the more mature of our merchants and businessmen are again supporting our paper. [8]

a direct reference to the fact that Eaton and his fellow Sophisticates and their supporters had not resumed advertising in the paper. Eaton clearly could not ignore the innuendo. His response was a letter to the paper making wild accusations, which the editor was easily able to refute in her editorial in the same issue, not least by quoting from a transcript of the programme. She went on to do him the indignity of publicly correcting his spelling. While in his letter he resorted to the Sophisticates' characteristic ritual tactic of legitimisation by portraying the protest as a 'unanimous' decision of the *Chamber of Commerce* (he being a mere member) and the town council, she exposed the extent of his personal involvement:

Eaton called a meeting of the merchants of the town.

and noted that while all those *present* may have supported his move,

... only eleven members out of a total of thirty-four attended—hardly, in our opinion, a 'unanimous' decision when less than one third of the Chamber's members were present. [9]

His penultimate paragraph was devoted to a vicious attack on the elementary school Principal, and earned him—Eaton was then Chairman of the School Board and thus the Principal's employer—a properly contemptuous reply. And, he ended,

This letter is written without consultation with any other businessmen and represents the personal views of the writer . .

to which the editor brusquely retorted,

It is heartening to know that Mr Eaton speaks only for himself . . .

For once, the Sophisticate had emerged from his organisational cocoon and been roundly beaten. His self-interest (as a businessman) had been exposed, as had his attempt to hide behind the Legitimisers. Even his *minority* support among the businessmen had come to light. Indeed, his overestimation of his support amongst the businessmen is a good indication of his ignorance of local political allegiances and of the extent to which he misinterprets the local political idiom. Finally, he suffered the indignity of having his behaviour shown to be ridiculous and petty.

Eaton had attempted to indulge in a personal campaign—precisely the kind in which the People's Group activists, and particularly Thomas Rodgers, would have delighted. He had shown a total lack of understanding of such a strategy, and had thus exhibited the extent of his estrangement from the more traditional and culturally legitimate modes of articulation.[10] As such, he had gone out on a limb as the meritocratic modernist and harbinger of change, disguising his interests as being those of the community, and had been humiliated in the eyes of the other community activists. But such is his standing and known influence in the various community organisations that his humiliation must be reflected in them as well. Whilst his defeat may not have been recognised by the less literate public, it became a powerful instrument in the hands of the People's Group activists: they could point to the particularistic interests of the Sophisticate organisations and causes. And it is noteworthy that in the issue of the paper in which the argument was conducted there were no advertisements for any of the Sophisticates' businesses or for those of their peripheral activists; however, both the Martins and Lester did advertise, as did some of their supporters.

The contrast between these styles of articulation as strategies of myth management is clear. The People's Group activists' insistent use of the personal approach is paralleled by the Sophisticates' employment of the organisational medium, the one representing tradition, the other modernity. It should be noted, though, that whilst the People's Group's strategies exploit traditionalism, they are applied to situations in which some socio-economic change is sought—albeit change of a different and much slower variety than that favoured by the Sophisticates. But as traditionalism employed to achieve and legitimate change, the People's Group's characteristic mode of articulation is syncretistic and culture-extending; as modernity used to achieve change, the Sophisticates' articulation is culture-substituting.

In terms of the 'development' of the community, the conflict may again be seen to be structurally marginal (Costa Pinto, 1965). The People's Group's insistence on the effectiveness of its—particularly Lester's—brokerage activities discourages 'grass-roots' attempts to communicate directly with the Government. As such, it prohibits the local citizen's transition from subject to participant in communal and governmental decision-making. But neither does the Sophisticates' organisational approach, with its connotations of exclusiveness and self-interest, do anything to encourage this transition. The community organisation seeks to provide services for the community, but it does not ask the community what it wants and neither does it invite communal participation in pursuit of the goal. In the rare organisational instances—of which the Economic Development Association was one—in which a degree of participation is sought, it is deterred by the domination of the organisation by successful businessmen to whom motives of self-interest and exploitation are imputed and who represent a departure from traditional values. Thus, on the one hand, participation is discouraged by being made unnecessary; and on the other hand, may be sought, but only in circumstances with which the citizen cannot identify.

Again, then, one notices that the conflict between the groups is not about *vertical* political change, with respect to the resources of leadership, but concerns *horizontal* change and the distribution of the resources of legitimacy among the few actors occupying the level of leadership. Further, it may be seen how the strategic modes of articulation imply the myths which constitute the groups' respective claims for legitimacy: on the one hand, the continuation of customary practice as manifest in the People's Group's cultural extension; on the other, the desirability of change, as suggested by the Sophisticates' culture-substituting organisational posture.

NOTES TO CHAPTER FIVE

[1] In a sample of the Herring Bay population I surveyed in 1969, 36·7 per cent (55) claimed to have met their Member of the House of Assembly; 17·3 per cent (26) had met both their Member and their federal M.P.

[2] Parts of this section appear in Cohen and Comaroff (forthcoming).

[3] While this consideration does not dispute the assymetry frequently postulated for the patron-client relation, it does tend to qualify the assumption of Paine (1971)

98   The management of myths

et al. that the values circulating in the relation are of the patron's choosing: they may well have been dictated by the broker.

[4] See Horwood (1967) for a superb character sketch.

[5] Indeed, the depopulation of regional centres such as Focaltown is a problem of which the potential in Newfoundland has often been noted. See, *inter alia*, Evans (1966, 13–14); Wadel (1969, 85).

[6] I understand this mine closed in 1972, but that the company was surveying locally for a new mine.

[7] This position was created at my suggestion. The idea was seized on by Eaton as a means of legitimating his presidency.

[8] *Focaltown News*, 27 February 1969.

[9] *Focaltown News*, 27 March 1969.

[10] In this regard, Eaton provides evidence for Bailey's conclusion that 'men destroy themselves not always because they have to in order to defend a principle, but sometimes because they have not learned how to communicate through confrontations and how to keep their encounters socially inexpensive' (1969, 224).

CHAPTER SIX

Myth management in the production of support

So far I have suggested that the competitive struggle for legitimacy is inherent in the characteristics of group membership, and in the groups' respective political objectives and modes of articulation. In this chapter I discuss the ways in which the leaders employ the strategies of myth management through which they seek legitimacy, to produce active support and supporters at various 'levels' of society. The People's Group seeks support at three levels—the government, the public, and among peripheral activists. The Sophisticates are concerned with the first and third of these (see Figure 2).

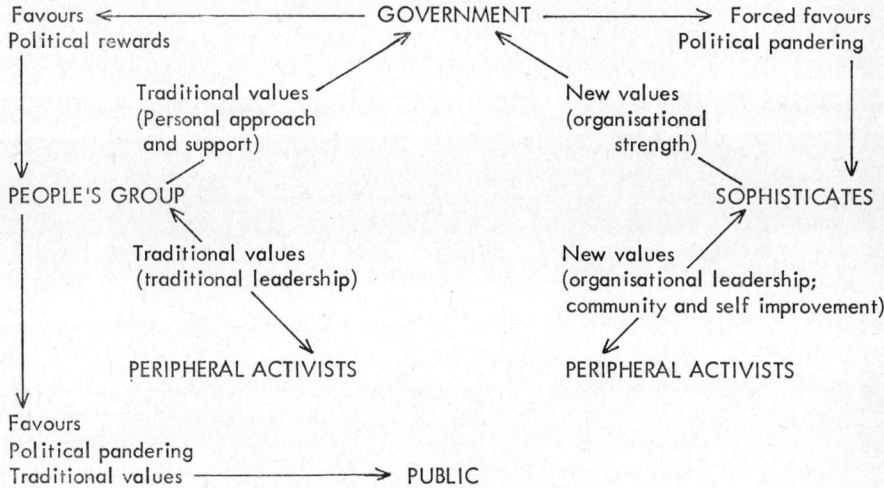

Figure 2. Vehicles of support mobilisation

THE GROUPS' ANTAGONISM AS IDEOLOGICAL CONFLICT

I would suggest that the groups' strategic approaches to the production of support underlines the ideological and cultural cleavage which separates them. Such an emphasis is necessary, for it could be argued that the antagonisms which inform the politics of leadership in Focaltown are reducible to the incompatibility of personalities and career ambitions. If, for example, the differences between the myth managing strategies of the Sophisticates and the People's Group did not extend beyond the group members themselves to their peripheral activists, we might be justified in concluding that they were merely rooted in personal hostility and that the other characteristics distinguishing the two groups were circumstantial and coincidental. I have even suggested at various points that the two groups have, in part, been forced to their antagonistic stances by the exigencies of their competition. We know, further, that there was some hostility between the Martins and Wayne Eaton before the latter moved to Focaltown and engineered the demise of their commercial and political ascendancy (see chapter 3). Is it not possible that their political contest is just an extension of their commercial rivalry? Similarly, we may use the evident rivalry between Donald Farrar and Stan Lester to bring the significance of the conflict into question. The issue may be quite simple: Lester wants the Liberal Party's nomination for the candidacy for Herring Bay. He perceives in Farrar not simply a rival who is more intelligent than he is, but also one who has established himself provincially as a figure of public importance. He also perceives in him one who now has two institutional bases from which to approach the local communities both as broker and, even, as patron. As President of the Herring Bay Economic Development Association, Farrar may not only purvey requests from the locality to the government: he may also mediate them. With perfect justification, he may choose which messages to transmit and which to support. As a broker, he could become vital to the community seeking to have its case presented. Secondly, as Superintendent of the Herring Bay Consolidated School Board, he has patronage at his disposal. He advises the board on its policy and priorities. He has money to allocate to the various communities for their schools. Through his authority to decide whether or not a community will get a teacher he is critical to the very survival of these communities. Farrar was ambitious, and known to be so. But at the time this study was made, he suffered from three disadvantages. Firstly, he was clever; he was described typically as 'smart', a label which is a liability in Focaltown, for it suggests that he puts, or would put his intelligence at the service of his self-satisfaction. Moreover, of course, it suggests that he is different—he is set apart, both by his recognised intelligence and by his educational achievements. The second disadvantage was that he was young, and had built an impressive career very quickly. This suggested to the local people firstly, that he was aggressively ambitious and, secondly, that his ambition was tied up with a pernicious self-interest: not surprisingly, perhaps, Focaltowners seem to assume that ambition or self-interest can be served only at the expense of others. The third disadvantage was partly a consequence of the first two: he could not talk to the local public in their own idiom. If he talked naturally, it was a 'different language', on a different level. If he tried to talk their language he was regarded as being patronising, and anyway it sounded unnatural. But then, quite suddenly, he was able to step into the two roles which gave him patronal bases from which to approach the public: the superintendency of the educational district, and the presidency of the Economic Development Association. He was no longer just the self-seeking young man; he had things to give people and to do for them.

This could well have given Stan Lester cause for anxiety. If so, he might have set out to discredit Farrar, and to oppose him at every opportunity. If the conflict between the Martins and Wayne Eaton can be explained by their commercial rivalry, why not explain the juxtaposition of Lester and Farrar in terms of their political jealousies and objectives?

My answer is twofold. In the first place, the validity of such an explanation would not contradict, but only complement one which took account of the complexities of Focaltown politics. There are, indeed, deep-rooted personal animosities between the groups of activists, but they are set within the context of the *ideologically* based conflict: the distinguishing attitudes and myth-managing styles of the groups are sufficiently constant to permit the derivation of an ideology—of change—from each. These ideologies suggest the terms in which the competing groups seek legitimacy for their styles of leadership—styles of which the legitimacy is rendered problematic by their departure from the traditional norm. Thus, the People's Group manages syncretic myths; the Sophisticates manage 'substitutive' myths. Syncretism suggests merely the 'modernisation' of the *status quo*, whilst cultural substitution demands its replacement. The ideologies validate the horizontal political change—the redistribution of the resource of legitimacy among the leaders of Focaltown's community life. Secondly, whilst the ideological confrontation may embrace, and even derive from personal animosities, the conflict is becoming routinised: it has become so deeply rooted in political process in Focaltown that it now transcends the individuals who comprise the two groups. It has spread through the organisations and into the religious denominations. It has created a new set of political activists—peripheral to the main conflict and its parties—in whom it will presumably endure until such time as it may be recognised that the ideologies of both are redundant and irrelevant. And, of course, it became closely paralleled at the provincial level, in the antic battle between Smallwood and the 'reform conservatives'.

I concentrate most of my attention in this chapter on these peripheral activists, and deal with the production of support at other societal levels rather more briefly.

THE PERIPHERAL ACTIVISTS

Each of the two groups has its peripheral activists, but by the nature of their composition and strategy, the Sophisticates have greater need of peripheral activism than does the People's Group: where the People's

Group activists have only their personalities, political images and such patronal obligations as they can muster to take into battle, the Sophisticates take their organisations. The effectiveness of the organisations obviously depends to a great extent on their ability to mobilise peripheral organisational activists into supportive roles. Most of the groups' peripheral activists belong to at least one of the principal organisations—the Lions Club, the Chamber of Commerce, the Canadian Legion, and the town council. But where the People's Group's peripheral activists are only incidentally members of these organisations, those who become peripheral activists in the Sophisticate cause do so by virtue of their participation in the organisations, one of which must be the Lions Club.

The People's Group's periphery
(i) The merchants

One element of the People's Group's supporting periphery shares largely in the characteristics which distinguish its elite group from the Sophisticates. They tend to be old-established businessmen who have been associated with the traditional leadership. Ideologically, they reflect the preferences of their leaders: traditionalistic, pro-Smallwood, 'indigenist'. They are not, by and large, intensively involved in the everyday business of community leadership, and they are not actively or constantly partisan. Rather, they constitute a residual pool of support which can be mobilised by the People's Group when the need arises. I have noted their association with the traditional leadership. To this may be added the traditionalism of their commercial *personae*: they present themselves as customary retail merchants rather than as aggressive entrepreneurs. Their images in this respect are managed in deliberate contrast to those of the 'businessmen' of the Sophisticate galaxy. They are most frequently mobilised by the manipulation of their traditionalism and their consequent resentment of Sophisticate innovation and ascendancy.

(ii) The Pentecostalist lay leaders

There is a second element in the People's Group's periphery whose presence there requires rather more attention. To an increasing extent the lay leaders of the Pentecostal Assembly appear amongst this group of activists. I have already dealt with several circumstantial reasons for the Pentecostalists' support of the People's Group. In addition to these, we might note that the People's Group's activists were considerably aided in the mobilisation of Pentecostalist support by the apparent reluctance of the Pentecostalists to elect one of their own number to a position of secular authority. Whilst there is clearly status differential within the Assembly, a curious egalitarianism dictates that it remain within sectarian boundaries and should not be perceived by those outside the Assembly. The social correlates of Pentecostalism are those of low socio-economic status (cf. Wilson, 1967, 141–2, n. 2), and in this area of Newfoundland, receipt of welfare. To some extent this is explained by the class appeal of evangelicalism. But—perhaps more important—it is, firstly, the consequence of the communality of the denomination: it is a community with closed boundaries in which one may seek security and obscurity in the company of people who have shared the same worldly experience of negligible opportunity, poverty, and a limited knowledge of the social environment. It is a society into which people may withdraw having felt misplaced or displaced in the secular world. Wadel has noted (1969*b*) that conversion to Pentecostalism may constitute one of the phases of status-passage from employed wage-earner to unemployed welfare-recipient in Newfoundland communities. Certainly in Focaltown there is some evidence that membership of the Assembly would be sought by unemployed men after a period of social seclusion following their transition to unemployment. As I have suggested, the 'closed' boundaries of the congregation offer the aderhent protection from the outside world. The religious device of public confession absolves him from feelings of guilt about his worldly situation. The similarity of the congregants' circumstances and their encapsulation produces a bond of solidarity amongst them.

Furthermore, it is a religion in which the experiences of the present world are made bearable by being made trivial: this life is simply a preparation for one much more important—and sweet—which will follow. Such a consolation will be valued since the unemployed man in rural Newfoundland has little opportunity to ameliorate his situation. Moreover, it offers him an escape from the competitive status-seeking of the material culture in which he is isolated and frustrated by his poverty. 'Secular' status is rhetorically denigrated within the Assembly. Rather, status is ascribed on the basis of 'religious' criteria as manifest, for example, in one's virtuosity at speaking in tongues. As Wilson points out (1967, 154),

Pentecostalists never weary of debunking worldly social status and of emphasising the unqualified significance of election by the Holy Ghost as the only status which really matters.

If, then, the adherent should seek to rise above his fellows in the secular sphere, he may be seen to be denying the communality wrought by shared experience; and secondly, a demonstration of instrumental interest in the affairs of this world may indicate a lack of faith in the superiority—and perhaps even the inevitability—of the next. Whether the pretexts are rooted more in doctrine or in social considerations, the Pentecostalists have traditionally looked for their political leaders outside their own sect. In Focaltown the circumstantial reasons alluded to oriented them towards the People's Group whose sympathetic stance and willing grasp of the constituency provided by the Assembly have reinforced the effect of the Pentecostalists' application of secular equalitarianism to the assumption of leadership roles.

The Pentecostalists' resentment of their co-religionists' attempts to secure leadership status in the community may be gauged from their recent voting behaviour. At the 1969 municipal election three Pentecostalists were candidates, one of them for re-election. None were elected. Indeed, as table 3 shows, two of them recorded their lowest polls in district 4—the Pentecostalist-dominated east end of town—one of them coming bottom of the poll there. The incumbent councillor recorded his worst poll in district 3, but his vote in district 4 was well below his overall average.

Table 3. Pentecostalist candidates' positions in poll and percentages of votes, by polling district: Focaltown municipal election, November 1969

	A		B		C	
	Position	%	Position	%	Position	%
Overall	8	6·83	10	4·74	12	4·12
District 1 'West end'; new subdivision; executives and affluents	8	6·66	7	6·82	11	5·33
District 2 Town centre; old-established families; Methodists and Anglicans	9	6·77	13	3·61	11	4·36
District 3 Pentecostalist fringe; Salvationists	7	7·85	11	4·73	13	2·58
District 4 'East end'; Pentocastalist concentration	10	5·61	15	2·51	13	3·29

We have seen that the People's Group, and specifically Stan Lester, exploited the Pentecostalists' predisposition to support him by campaigning against the Sophisticates in the general area of education. He further adroitly used their sensitivity to the threat of educational rights to secure their support for Smallwood in the leadership campaign. Ironically, the Smallwood campaign also reaped benefit from the high incidence of people on welfare. Smallwood has traditionally made his pitch as the man who brought the benefits of the welfare state to Newfoundland and, quite apart from the 'gratitude' he may have earned, there is also a tendency among welfare recipients to feel that welfare may be received 'only during good political behaviour': it may be taken away just as easily as it was given. DeWitt (1969, 44) describes the same phenomenon on Fogo Island, in the Notre Dame Bay region of the Province:

> ... there is a widespread belief on the island that criticism of the government, especially through the 'improper' use of the ballot, could result in the withdrawal of welfare ...

The Pentecostalists thus have an interest in the maintenance of the political *status quo*. They can, therefore, be mobilised into support of the People's Group and its objectives by depiction of the Sophisticates' activities and allegiances as constituting a threat to this *status quo*. The effectiveness of that strategy may be demonstrated by the fact that, with the exception of the chairman—Stan Lester—all of the executive members of the Action-for-Joey Committee were Pentecostalists, among them the Assembly's lay leaders—the Chairman of the Pentecostal School Board and the Principal of its high school. The Assembly condoned this instance of their participation in secular leadership since its object was to protect the interests of the congregation as a whole.

Apart from providing a source of mass support, the Pentecostalists also, then, 'second' their lay leaders to the People's Group's cause as peripheral activists. Their activity has become much more overt since the Liberal Party established its formal local Association, and is particularly noticeable since the Assembly proscribes participation in the Lions Club, boycotts the Chamber of Commerce, and recognises the town council as the only legitimate political-administrative institution in the community.

I am not suggesting that the Pentecostal Assembly is the only base of electoral support for the People's Group: rather, I am saying that it provides stable and mobilisable support which is not provided by any other denominational group in the community. Further, the support of other denominational adherents for the People's Group is not accountable as a characteristic of those denominations, but as consequences of their greater cultural and ideological affinity with the People's Group, their resentment of the Sophisticates' rapid ascendancy in the community, and the threat posed by it to the political *status quo*.

In this respect, we may see the People's Group mobilising support by pandering to the political sensibilities of the public and its leaders among the periphery of community activists. In the same way, we saw Thomas Rodgers discredit the Sophisticates and support Stan Lester's successful bids for the delegacy to the national Liberal leadership convention and for the presidency of the Herring Bay District Liberal Association. In each case he manipulated symbols and managed myths to which the public attributes great salience *and* sees as being threatened by the ascendancy of the Sophisticates: in the first case, loyalty to the *'livyer'*—indigene—and deference to the traditional leader; in the second, the political legitimacy of Smallwoodism and of the 'common man'. These symbols are clearly relevant to the production of support both amongst the peripheral activists and the public.

In sum, the peripheral activists of the People's Group may be seen to be generally mobilised by the manipulation of symbols associated with traditional political values, and by the identification of the danger to those values posed by threats to the predominance of the traditional political leadership.

The Sophisticates' periphery

The Sophisticates' peripheral activists tend to fall into three occupational categories. The first type are successful businessmen who, like the elite group members themselves, have moved into Focaltown from other communities. A second type are senior employees of local businesses who have proven their interest in community affairs by their participation in Lions Club activities. The third variety are senior employees of the Sophisticates' leader who, as such, are 'encouraged' to participate in community organisations. The first type are sufficiently like the Sophisticates themselves not to warrant separate discussion. I shall thus concentrate on the second and third, since it is precisely these activists, as a succeeding political 'generation', who represent the routinisation of the mythic and strategic conflict. These activists might be thought of as 'aspiring' leaders. But there was a further audience to which the Sophisticates addressed themselves, composed of a group of high school students. It is to this group that the Sopihsticates looked for succession, and I shall discuss the efficacy of their attempts to produce this support a little later.

(i) *The aspiring leaders*

It will be evident by now that whilst they acknowledge their vested interests in the community, the Sophisticates seek to justify their political behaviour at least partly on the grounds of 'community service'. In this ethic, the community becomes more than a collection of houses and people, and acquires a quasi-mystical status suggesting an object worthy of endeavour which is intrinsically good and self-fulfilling. 'Community service' and 'self-development' thus become synonymous, and comprise the myths managed by the Sophisticates. In order to be 'of use' to the Sophisticates, the peripheral activists must belong to a community organisation—inevitably, the Lions Club—for that is where their campaigns are waged. The very structure of the Lions Club lends itself to elite management. The individual is approached by a member and asked if he wishes to join. If he does, his application is reviewed at a directors' meeting, and its recommendation is passed on to the general Club membership. The Sophisticates are heavily entrenched on the Board of Directors, so they can easily enable the enrolment of their protégés. All of Wayne Eaton's senior employees, including the younger office staff, belong to the Club, largely through his persuasion or manipulation:

I am proud of the fact that [names his dozen leading employees] and I don't know how many others there were, they are all members of the Lions Club and ... I haven't told them they should be. *I have certainly, though, made it convenient* for them to join the Club because I would like for them to take part in the community.

Further, the Sophisticates seek to retain an oligarchical control of the Club:

I always suggest to the president when he mentions the nominating committee for the officers for next year that it be the ex-presidents who form the committee so that they can see to it that the right fellows stay with the executive all the time, so that fellows like myself can have a voice in it. Because if you don't, then the continuity of thought seems to break down, and if you get a vocalist, a chap who is radical and a vocalist, he can cause a lot of problems.

Thus, the activists are carefully screened as they enter the arena, and the upward progress of their careers is largely contingent on Sophisticate favour. Along with the ethics of Lionism—self-fulfilment through community leadership and service—goes the acknowledgement of the real hierarchy of control, including deference and emulation among the peripheral activists. Discussing his influence in the Club, Wayne Eaton understates his resources, but indicates the typical Sophisticate ethic of the proven right to lead:

They recognise my ability of having done something [i.e. built a successful business] and they want leadership . . . they just want ideas to work on . . .

The elitist connotations of the Club bestow some prestige on its initiates, which appears to be particularly valued by those who are not self-employed: it gives them status amongst their occupational peers and brings them regularly into a temporarily 'equalitarian' relationship with their employers. As a consequence, one finds the most enthusiastic younger Lions among the employees of the largest local employers—Eaton's, Martin's, and —— Mining Company; suggesting that the larger and more amorphous the peer group, the greater is the desire to establish a valued and distinguishing identity. Banfield (1958, 85) explains voluntary association membership in the United States in similar terms:

Those who belong to 'do-good' organisations secure gratifications [e.g. status, power, neighbourly association, etc.] which have nothing to do with the public-spirited purposes for which the organisations exist.

The initiate clearly cannot express such values explicitly as a rationale for his participation in the Club, so others are made available. There is, firstly, the Club's self-image as a service organisation; and secondly, the portrayal of community service as the path to 'self-development', which is held to be intrinsically good. The Sophisticates attract to themselves the young, ambitious, and upwardly mobile would-be activists of Focaltown, by posing as the personifications of these values. As such, they portray support of themselves as being inherently edifying and educative, and talk of mobilising the activists for their own good. This paternalism is particularly evident in Eaton's description of his attitude towards his employees:

I owe it to them to . . . make sure that they are good citizens and all.

Three years previously, his firm had borne 70 per cent of the costs of running a Dale Carnegie course in the town,

> ... and I was able to get fourteen of our employees to take it ... I was proud of this and all in the effort ... to make them better citizens.

Both of the competing leadership groups tend to mobilise their peripheral activists into actively opposed alignments only when a critical issue is topical. Because of their organisational base, the Sophisticates' supporters tend to be easily mobilised. Peripheral activism in Focaltown thus permits us to see what the configuration of future leadership might be like if there was no significant change at the grass-roots level, and if the groups were successful in producing the kinds of support they sought. Within the community's sphere of activism, the mythic political style of the People's Group would seem to have no heirs: their peripheral activists are either of the same generation of leaders or have limited interests. The younger activists, who tend to Sophisticate styles, would therefore have a monopoly of the leadership roles, other than those occupied by the Legitimisers. That would indeed represent some change in the politics of leadership. Participation at grass-roots level would not increase, since Sophisticate politics is elite-based and rooted in socially exclusive organisations and attributes. Here, I again reiterate my argument that the Sophisticates' passage to legitimated leadership would not imply any change in the vertical political relationship of leaders and the mass. Social change in the Focaltown context would thus seem to sustain, rather than to threaten, political elitism.

We may summarise the values which the Sophisticates manipulate to produce support amongst these peripheral activists to be, typically, culturally alien: they stress the virtues of community service and self-improvement, virtues which are held to find their synthesis in organisational leadership.

(ii) *The anti-leaders*[1]

The active use which the Sophisticates make of their periphery, particularly of its younger members, goes some way towards indicating their concern with the production of successors. In part, this concern may be explained by the proof successors would offer of the routinisation—and, therefore, by implication, of the sound establishment—of Sophisticate ascendancy. But the elevation of these activists into positions of public prominence would also have the effect of validating Sophisticate myths of meritocratic mobility, organisational endeavour, and the benefits of 'community service'. But such myths of 'achievement' would gain their most spectacular substantiation from the successful careers of Focaltown children, and particularly from those who could be shown to have benefited from Sophisticate activity. For this reason, perhaps, the Sophisticates sought an audience among a small group of senior students in the amalgamated high school, the school in the establishment and administration of which they had been so intimately and conspicuously involved. The children are not, of course, involved as activists in community leadership; but they are *potentially*, and for that reason and because of the attention which the Sophisticates consequently pay to them I include them briefly in the present discussion.

The children—eight in number—are closely associated with the community's leadership through kinship or other parental ties. Their ascriptive and meritocratic attributes mark them out as heirs-apparent to the community's leadership. They are courted by the Sophisticates on three counts. In a community in which the politics of leadership is so intensive that it pervades all levels of social organisation, they are, in themselves, important sources of approval and support. Secondly, they serve as key elements—exemplars—in the leaders' rhetoric. And thirdly, as they reach an age to enter the arena of leadership, they would become potential activists in the Sophisticate cause and must therefore be protected, as resources, from the influence of the People's Group.

I am conscious here, as throughout this study, of the danger of exaggerating the activists' consciousness of their competitive relationships with each other and, therefore, of painting their entire social behaviour in terms of strategic considerations and unremitting calculation. I do not suggest that there is a planned campaign with respect to the indoctrination of the children. It is simply the case that they did attract extraordinary attention from the Sophisticates which is accountable both in terms of Sophisticate mythology and of the competitive struggle for legitimacy.

The children were among the brightest of the graduating students, and some of them were obvious candidates for admission to university. With two exceptions, they are related to the Sophisticates themselves or to their associates. They are frequently subjected to Sophisticate mythology as they receive the leaders' 'confidences' with respect to Focaltown politics. The Sophisticates justify their political campaigns to the youngsters as being for *their* benefit—the construction of a modern school, the provision of recreational facilities, the general enhancement of community life. They are lectured on the morality of meritocratic achievement and the infinite superiority of the 'new' North American milieu over the parochial isolation and backwardness of the past. They are admonished to take their places in the world as a new generation of leaders, to seize the available opportunities to gain access to positions of achieved prominence.

To all of this—and for reasons I have discussed in detail elsewhere (Cohen, 1975b)—the children turn cynical and apathetic ears. Their aspirations are to live and work in the Focaltown area, for whose employment market they are now overeducated; they have to leave. They are uneasily aware of the contradictions within Focaltown between the material affluence of the entrepreneurial age, and the desolation wrought by unemployment in a society largely dependent upon the welfare cheque.

They also recognise the extent to which these 'two communities' have been polarised by the struggle for legitimacy between the two groups of leaders. They therefore reject the political activity urged upon them by the Sophisticates, not through positive dissent or protest, but through a feeling of being misplaced in, and displaced by, the kind of world depicted in Sophisticate mythology. They resign themselves to the futility of participation and revert to the traditional adult preoccupation with the protection —rather than active pursuit—of individualistic self-interest. The Sophisticates' attempt to produce support amongst the children has culminated only in the production of a group of 'anti-leaders'.

Ironically, the Sophisticates' failure to produce support among these potential leaders underlines their likely success with the organisational periphery. The children have many ways in which they can compete to rise above their peers without restorting to the advertisement of their associations with a group of adults who are widely regarded with suspicion. They can distinguish themselves academically or athletically. But the young activists, the aspiring leaders, are obliged to seek their public reputations within the highly competitive organisational milieu created and dominated by the Sophisticates. It is hardly surprising that access to such valued reputations should lie through recognised association with Sophisticate endeavour. The Sophisticates thus produce support among a periphery of activists who are their political dependents; they fail among the generation which has no further need of them.

THE PRODUCTION OF HIGHER LEVEL SUPPORT

We have seen already that the People's Group activists articulate with the government largely through the medium of the personal approach. Coupling this with professions of political loyalty, which we have seen to be demonstrated in intra-party campaigns, they attempt to mobilise governmental support in the same way. Given the declining resources of patronage—services such as roads, electricity, water supply, mains sewerage, and telephones—it is a loyalty which must occasionally and, one may hypothesise, increasingly go unrequited. More often now the government responds with political rewards for the activists themselves; they are cheaper. Hence, we have seen that Mr Smallwood helped the election of Stan Lester to the presidency of the local district Liberal Association, and possibly also to become delegate to the National Liberal leadership convention. He also enables him to maintain his image as an effective broker in the outlying settlements. It is consistent with their greater traditionalism that the People's Group should go to the government seeking aid for the community politely and regarding it as a favour rather than as a right. Contrasting the efficacy of this strategy with the ruder approach of the Sophisticate organisations, Stan Lester said,

... there is a tendency within groups like that, rather than politely ask for something, to feel that the government has a responsibility to them—like this pavement [i.e. the hardsurfacing of Focaltown's approach road]: they think the government has a responsibility to a community this size to provide this pavement. But this is an outright gift from the government ... there is lots of places looking for the same things as us. If you don't have the right approach ... members of the government can just as easily say 'no' as they can 'yes'. I think good relationships with these people is very, very important.

His characterisation of the Sophisticates' attitude is accurate. Whilst the People's Group trades with the government on traditional values of supplication and, to some extent, of exchange, the Sophisticates employ the contextually new values of organisational strength. They appear not simply as the representatives of particular interests but, rather, as an organised and powerful pressure group which denies the continued legitimacy of the traditional approach. Therefore, they do indeed demand satisfaction as a right rather than as a favour; they do not offer values in return.

At a more basic level, the Sophisticates react with indignation to the People's Group's activists' assertions of the efficacy of their individualistic approaches. A public confrontation between Donald Farrar and Stan Lester occurred when, after the Chamber of Commerce had decided to invite a certain notable personality in the Province to be a guest speaker, Lester suggested that he should make the approach through one of his 'friends' in the government. Farrar's response was vehemently to assert the integrity of the organisation, and,

... if he won't come for the Chamber, then we don't want him to come for his friends.

a remark which adequately expresses the Sophisticate attitude.

I have already exemplified the Sophisticates' characteristic use of organisations as media in their relations with the government. But the important point to notice in this context is that not only are their approaches impersonal, they also involve the exertion of pressure rather than the more traditional supplication. An important example concerned the paving of Focaltown's access road to the Trans-Canada Highway, referred to by Stan Lester in the quotation above. In 1958 the premier had publicly promised to have the road paved. Ten years and three general elections passed and the road still retained its gravel surface. Then, shortly before the Federal elections in 1968, the Chamber of Commerce published an open letter to the premier in the Provincial press, including in it a newspaper report of the ten-year-old promise, and saying that it had resorted to this action since its previous requests had met with no response. A few days later the premier arrived in Focaltown, apparently uttering condemnations of treachery. Perhaps as a result of the inadvisability of having one's political credibility questioned just before a general election, road-paving operations began shortly after and were completed before the summer was out. The strategy was one which the People's Group could not, and would not, have espoused. In their view, the *request* was legitimate; the *demand* was not. But, the personal delegation of old had given way to the relative anonymity of the bureaucrats' typewriter.

THE PRODUCTION OF PUBLIC SUPPORT

It will be evident from my discussion of the characteristic modes of articulation that the Sophisticates do not generally attempt to produce active support among the public. Indeed, their entrepreneurial ethic demands that the implementation of policies formulated by the 'middle-class' organisations should not be constrained by the requirements of public approval and participation. Their manifest concern to limit the impingement of the public will was clear in the constitutional arrangements they formulated for the Economic Development Association. I have remarked also on their social and cultural distance from Focal-towners, which obviously inhibits any attempts to seek an affirmation of support by the public that they might feel inclined to make. Their public electoral successes have been negligible. John Whiteway was a councillor in the days when Edward Martin nominated the candidates and ensured that his nominees would be unopposed. In 1961, on the only occasion that Wayne Eaton has been a candidate for council, he came bottom of the poll. Donald Farrar has been sufficiently aware of his electoral disadvantages to restrain himself from becoming a candidate for the council or local parliamentary seats. Ivan Lush is the only Sophisticate who currently serves on council and, as I have already suggested, his success is not adequately explained by his personal popularity. One might add that he twice unsuccessfully contested the Herring Bay provincial parliamentary division, in 1971 and 1972, and lost both times. On the latter occasion Herring Bay was one of only nine seats which did not fall to the Progressive Conservatives.

The Sophisticates' concern with their legitimisation is not, therefore, paralleled by any determined attempt to produce manifest support amongst the public. Their own legitimisation would also involve the validation of the Sophisticate Idea, which suggests the justification of elite, exclusive and bureaucratic leadership unfettered by considerations of uninformed popular participation.

The People's Group, of course, depends upon manifest public support for the affirmation of its legitimacy, in its political relation with the Sophisticates—the relation in which legitimacy itself is the unequally distributed and valued resource. Indeed, the claims of the People's Group activists to legitimacy are largely based upon the putative popularity of their values. I have already described at length the ways in which they attempt to portray their affinity to—perhaps, even, personification of—these values. From the foregoing discussion we may conclude that, in so far as they prevail over the Sophisticates with regard to the scarce resource of legitimacy, the People's Group activists can only sustain their positions by producing concrete public support. The ways in which they seek such support may be briefly summarised, or inferred, from the material already presented.

We have noted that Lester's electoral support in Focaltown is not very great. Clearly, a substantial proportion of his vote may be attributed to the Pentecostalist population and to his many relatives. I would suggest that the remainder of his support derives, firstly, from his known association with Thomas Rodgers, and secondly, from whatever 'popularity' he may have acquired as the proprietor of one of the town's public bars. The former resource may be translated into mobilisation through the values of traditional leadership. The second is anybody's guess: before the 1969 election, he was said to have made some attempts to convert the debts of three of his clients into political obligations but one may only speculate on the extent and success of such strategies. Outside of Focaltown, he clearly mobilises support through his 'brokerage' activities. Quite simply, he does favours—or appears to do so—in anticipation of support.[2]

In their attempts to mobilise support among the public Thomas Rodgers and Arthur Martin exploit the institutional and ascriptive bases of their legitimacy. Rodgers always made great play of his intimacy with Smallwood—the implication being that if Smallwood was sitting on the 'public chest' (cf. Gwyn, 1968, 125; Perlin, 1971; 1972), he might always dip into it for his friends. He also had the prestige and legitimacy which attaches to public office in Newfoundland. As mayor for twenty years, he became the beneficiary of that quirk of Newfoundland political culture which bestows legitimacy on the incumbent as well as on the role. There is a cultural disinclination to question or challenge authority, which tends to maintain incumbents in office.[3] Rodgers also acquired legitimacy from his associations with the community's traditional leadership. His performance was such that he became a legitimate leader 'in his own right', to the extent that association with him has become a means of 'borrowing' legitimacy.

Arthur Martin benefits from associations similar to those of Rodgers, both ascriptively—as the merchant's eldest son—and institutionally—as a long-serving councillor and mayor. Like his two People's Group colleagues, his managerial or presentational strategies are designed to extend the legitimacy won in different historical circumstances to the contemporary structural and cultural situation.

In sum, we may conclude that the People's Group activists produce support amongst the public, as amongst the peripheral activists, by managing myths of traditional leadership, by pandering to the peculiar interests of particular groups, and by 'demonstrating' their efficacy as brokers.

The values which the groups employ to produce support thus appear to be dichotomous. On the one hand, they are traditional—soliciting and rewarding; on the other, they are alien—demanding, and asserting the inherent reward entailed in acceptance of the values.

But as with the other strategic aspects of their struggle for legitimacy, the groups' myth-managing strategies have in common that neither seeks the redistribution of political resources between the level of leadership and the non-activist public. The antagonists' concern to limit or contain the dissemination of leadership resources provides a 'frame' for their ritual confrontation. The traditional, culture-extending elite seeks to create its own indispensability, not by emphasising the goods it can *itself* provide, but rather by demonstrating its grace with those on high. In so doing it implicitly asserts the inutility of the population's organisation for 'self-help'. The strategy is evident in other familistic or atomised communities, whose lack of communality may be attributed partly to the structures of dependency created and maintained by the interests of patronage (e.g. Banfield, 1958; Silverman, 1965). For their part, the Sophisticates indicate their awareness of the community by providing it with the services which they feel it ought to want. They impose their wills upon the public. But whilst their paternalism and neglect of popular support is consistent with the strategy of organisational domination, the extent to which it enhances the legitimacy of organisational and cognate values amongst the public is highly problematic.

The strategic production of support should therefore be seen as an aspect of competitive myth management whose basic rationale is the protection of the managers rather than the propagation of their mythic values.

NOTES TO CHAPTER SIX

[1]The material in the section which follows receives detailed discussion in Cohen (1975*b*).

[2]Cf. Blau (1964, 269) on 'social credit'.

[3]I would suggest in passing that the substantive achievement of John Crosbie's opposition to Smallwood, beginning with his resignation from the Cabinet in 1968 and culminating in his candidacy for the Liberal leadership in 1969, was to make challenge to established authority somewhat more legitimate, if only by making it more common.

CHAPTER SEVEN

The problem of legitimacy in Focaltown politics: conclusion

I have employed a model of myth to suggest the character of the legitimation processes manifest in the politics of Focaltown's leadership. I have suggested that through myth and its strategic management reference is made—either explicitly or implicitly—to a body of principles from which the values governing social organisation and social relations are drawn. In this sense, myth, like ritual, provides a bridge between the level of 'valued' reality—the 'sacred', the unquestioned—and the level of mundane process, informed by 'problems', at which dispute and contestation occur. In this functional respect, myth and ritual are means by which value is imparted to social relations, and it is in this attribution of values, postulated in terms of principles of justification, that legitimisation consists. The significance of legitimisation becomes apparent if we locate it within the broad range of *political* processes, in the diffuse senses I have earlier identified with 'politics'. We are dealing here with relations structured around the unequal distribution of a valued social resource. It might reasonably be asked how it is that we accept relations of inequality, of how we come to sanction the different behaviour of people holding differentiated statuses in systems of unequally distributed resources: in particular situations, and with respect to particular resources, we acknowledge *alter* to be in a superior position, and we permit him to behave accordingly, Opposing social theories and philosophies are largely constituted by their answers to these questions, whether couched in terms of proximity to economic power, consensual values, force, exchange, or whatever. But common to all such answers is the notion that we do not persistently question the structure of our social relationships because we have devices by which we keep their questionable aspects out of discussion. For Marx, these devices were manifest in 'false consciousness'; for Durkheim, many belong to religion; in Lévi-Strauss's sociology, they are provided by myth. All of these may be subsumed under the general rubric of legitimisation.

Such 'sacred' legitimated elements of social life are rarely articulated; they seldom require to be made explicit. They emerge in the intuitive responses we make in given social situations—that is, reactions which are directed by the basic values which need to be internalised for a particular system of order to be mainted. These are the kinds of values which we ordinarily speak of as being 'deep', 'communal', or 'shared' within a given culture. They are manifest, for example, in the Focaltowner's acceptance of the 'need' for leadership, that is, of his tolerance of an unequal relation in which he is generally the subservient actor. The problem of legitimacy which absorbs the contesting elites in Focaltown is not concerned with the legitimacy of the *fact* of leadership, but with the legitimacy of the *kinds* of leadership which should prevail. It is in precisely such a struggle that we may see the management of myth and ritual attempting to bridge the gap between a sacral or unquestioned mythic world—the values of leadership, or of being led—and the existential world of disputes about which particular styles of leadership are appropriate and 'culturally correct'. Both sets of myth-managers seek to depict the affinity of their own styles to those implicit in the valued and mythic order. The 'order' of cultural extension is somehow related to the traditional past; cultural substitution suggests a valued system in the cultural future.

In their efforts to gain legitimacy, both People's Group and Sophisticate activists exploit the residual values which validate the 'necessity' of leadership in Focaltown, that is to say, the values which justify and sustain the unequal relations of leaders and led. Some of these values have been frequently noticed by other writers and may be categorised as deference towards authority (Feltham, 1959, 33; Smith, 1968, 18; Evans, n.d., 12), reluctance to accept positions of leadership (Evans, 1966, part 2, 6; Faris, 1972; Gwyn, 1968, 125; Stiles, 1971; 1972; Wadel, 1971), and disinclination to organise collectively (Crosbie, 1956, 334; Wadel, 1969, 120; 1971, *passim*; Stiles, 1971; Copes, 1970). These values may be seen as the residual products of a history of repression, exploitation, and the unending struggle to wreak a living out of a frequently hostile environment.

In the context of the present leadership struggle in Focaltown, these values impinge upon the leaders' strategies in two ways. In the first place, they predispose the public to accept leadership and to refrain from participation in the management of their own social affairs. They enable the small number of actors at the level of leadership to monopolise leadership roles. But, secondly, they provide the terms in which the leaders' claims to legitimacy are evaluated by the public. They constitute the backdrop of political culture against which the present drama is acted out. They comprise the language which Focaltowners use to make the behaviour of leaders intelligible. These values, therefore, sustain the fact or institution of leadership, but at the same time they render problematic the legitimacy of particular styles of leadership.

DEFERENCE

In a recent discussion of the sociological literature on English political culture the argument has been made that there is '. . . a theory of deference in search of data', and that since the concept of deference is so hard to define and 'operationalise', it might fruitfully be abandoned (Kavanagh, 1971, 360). This argument seems to me to exemplify the way in which some social scientists' concern to find 'measures' leads them to neglect or misunderstand the societies and their phenomena that they seek to measure. There has to be room for intuition in the sociologists' enquiry— or, at least, recognition of its inevitability. Intuitively or otherwise, the characteristics that we colloquially associate with 'deference' seem to me to be inescapable to an observer of the Focaltown, and more generally, the rural Newfoundland population. It is, admittedly, a diffuse quality whose properties are difficult to specify, but is no less real for that. There is, for example, a widespread belief that any person standing in an authoritative relation to oneself is necessarily correct in his judgements, which should therefore be followed even if they conflict with one's own opinions. It is the readiness to defer to the judgements of social superiors which is so striking. A further dimension of Focaltown deference, rather more difficult to pin down to specific indices, is manifest in the humility and respect with which social superiors are approached. The relation of deference is not, though, given simply by social distance, but, rather, by a variety of subtle traditional evaluative signals centering mainly on the bases of *alter's* superiority and the manner of his behaviour.

I would suggest that the inclination to defer to authority is the product of two themes in Newfoundland culture: the first consists in particular structural conditions which have informed Newfoundland's social history, and the second becomes manifest in an idealised conception of political activism. The first theme is, perhaps, best described as conditioning to highly concentrated power. In the communities of Herring Bay, the control of social life was usually the exclusive property of two men—the merchant and the magistrate.[1] The traditional power of the merchant was such as to justify the description of rural Newfoundland as a mercantile feudality. Through the systems of truck and credit he was able to extend his domain into all spheres of the fisherman's life. I have mentioned already the extensive jurisdiction of the magistrate over the varied aspects of community organisation. He was the representative of a legal system which was for long based on arbitrary and repressive law, and was only gradually institutionalised and turned into a set of principles more easily recognisable as 'justice' in the British legal sense. The reverence for the magistrate's authority was perhaps a token of the protection he gave against a return to the barbarity and ruthlessness of earlier forms of legal agency.[2] Quite apart from the concentration of power at the local level, rural Newfoundlanders were attuned to powerlessness and political dependency by the centralisation of all administrative matters in the national government in St John's. There was no local government. There were no local representative institutions. Then as now the interrelations between the governmental and mercantile elites of St John's were so intimate as to be virtually inextricable (see Noel, 1971). In the post-Confederation era, the all-encompassing power of the government has been modernised rather than significantly reduced.

I suggest that these historical and structural conditions have induced in the Newfoundlander an enduring readiness to accept the dictates of authority, an attitude which has been sacralised and, until recently, appeared hardly to be questioned. The attitude was expressed succinctly by a Herring Bay housewife who, referring to both bureaucratic and elective authorities, told me that

They are there to rule us and make the rules for us. We should obey them.

to which her husband added,

The 'Book' says you should respect those in authority over you.

a nice, if rather, literal, example of the sacralisation of social arrangements. The typicality of such attitudes among the local population may be indicated by the responses given, in a survey conducted in 1969, to the question, 'Which do you believe is more important: to respect someone in a position of authority even if you disagree with him, or always to do what *you* think is right?' Table 4 shows the distribution of responses in two random samples, the first drawn from Herring Bay and an adjacent urban centre, and the second from Focaltown. 64·5 per cent of the first sample, and 77·8 per cent of the second, would defer to authority whilst disagreeing with its dictates; only 30·7 per cent and 19·4 per cent respectively, would follow their own inclinations.

Table 4. Distribution of responses indicating deference to authority as opposed to personal decision

Response	Herring Bay		Focaltown	
	N	%	N	%
Respect authority	252	64·5	28	77·8
Do what *you* think	120	30·6	7	19·4
Don't know	19	4·9	1	2·8
Total	391	100·0	36	100·0

The three structural factors mentioned above refer to systems of imposed authority. But as structures which induce deference, they were augmented by popular beliefs in the integrity and competence of elected and appointed officials: authority is regarded as the manifestation of superior intelligence matched by sincerity. We find the paradox that 'established' leaders—that is to say, those whose leadership has been legitimated—are regarded with some idealism, whilst those who seek to dislodge them are automatically assumed to be motivated by self-interest. This idealism extends to the evaluation of leaders treated as an 'abstract' genus. It is particularly striking since corruption—or, to put it mildly and euphemistically, 'conflict of interest'—has traditionally been almost overt in Newfoundland politics (see Noel, 1971). Thus, in a society in which imputations of self-interest are, as we have seen, commonly made to community activists (cf. Szwed, 1966, 137; DeWitt, 1969, 43), majorities of both our samples attributed altruism rather than self-seeking to both local and provincial politicians. Table 5 shows that, in answer to the question, 'Why do you think people volunteer for positions of leadership or perform some sort of public service?' 48·3 per cent of the first sample, and 55·5 per cent of the second suggest an altruistic motive; 30·9 per cent and 27·8 per cent respectively give primacy to self-interest.

Table 5. Distribution of responses attributing motives for public service

Response	Herring Bay		Focaltown	
	N	%	N	%
For public good	189	48·3	20	55·6
Self-interest	121	30·9	10	27·8
Both	66	11·8	4	11·0
Other	17	4·4	1	2·8
Don't know	18	4·6	1	2·8
Total	391	100·0	36	100·0

Even if we subsume the response indicating a combination of self-interest and altruism under that of self-interest, we find that it is still a minority response and, indeed, remains so in a further question testing the same values in respect of politicians, although in the first sample self-interest is imputed to a somewhat greater extent. (Table 6 shows response to the question, 'Do you believe that most politicians are in politics in order to serve the people, or that most politicians are mainly out for themselves?')

Table 6. Distribution of responses attributing motives to politicians

Response	Herring Bay		Focaltown	
	N	%	N	%
Serve the people	192	49·1	23	63·9
Out for themselves	148	37·9	11	30·5
Don't know	51	13·0	2	5·6
Total	391	100·0	36	100·0

This idealistic conception of politics was summed up neatly—if indignantly—by a Focaltown housewife:

Of course most politicians are in politics in order to serve the people. Why would anyone take a position for himself?

It may be partly because of this attribution of 'public spiritedness' to community leaders that criticism of, or challenge to incumbents of legitimate offices is often met with accusations about the critic's ambition and political or economic self-interest, and by an emotive defence of the accused.

There is, of course, nothing surprising in a finding which shows that more people evaluate their leaders positively than negatively. If, indeed, such favourable evaluations did not prevail, the system of leadership would be unlikely to survive. What is interesting though for our purposes is that this 'idealism' is not applied equally to the People's Group and to the Sophisticates. The more 'traditional' culture-extending leaders are seen to participate in the sacralised—and largely undefined—forms of leadership, whilst the Sophisticates are somehow perceived to be threatening this valued system of order—which is, of course, exactly what they are doing. Thus, in the competitive struggle for legitimacy, the benefits of this structural conditioning and idealistic conception of politics flow far more to the People's Group than to the Sophisticates. Firstly, deference is owed to the leader displaying *traditional* attributes of leadership; secondly, the disinclination to organise breeds suspicion of organisationally-based activism; and thirdly, Sophisticate assertiveness is seen precisely as a challenge to legitimate authority—and such a challenge is made even more repugnant by coming from 'outsiders'. (Indeed, we may explain the relatively high incidence of imputations of self-interest in the responses reported above to the fact that the questions did not distinguish between types of leader or role.) The reaction to criticism of culturally legitimate leaders is perhaps best explained by saying that it is also interpreted as criticism of the values on which legitimacy is predicated. The People's Group activists are thus accorded legitimacy; the Sophisticates are not.

The effect of such culturally induced reactions may be clearly seen in perception of the People's Group–Sophisticate competition. Accusations of self-interest attach far more to the Sophisticates than to the People's Group. Whilst Lester's political ambition is recognised, it is forgiven and treated as little more than a foible; but Wayne Eaton's suspected economic self-interest precludes the possibility of his securing popular approval and support. In 1961, long before his political and commercial organisations had achieved their present pre-eminence, Eaton ran for council and came bottom of the poll with a grand total of fifteen votes. As one Legitimiser relates,

... the explanation I gathered from questioning people ... was that the majority of them said that the people in the town just didn't trust him, that they were afraid that if he got in there he'd take the town for everything it had—you know, he'd be out after his own interest.

Eaton's own explanation was that in his manifesto he had stated the necessity of raising taxes:

... I certainly wasn't surprised at the defeat because ... I was the only person who mentioned taxes when I wrote out my manifesto ... So I didn't get elected. I guess it was on account of my honesty.

The established leader is clearly very much harder to discredit than his aspiring successor.

The Sophisticates react to their lack of cultural legitimacy by rejecting the values in which legitimacy traditionally inheres. They try, for example, to obscure the resentful deference paid to them by disclaiming their right to, or desire for, deference. They thus tend to indulge in hearty back-slapping and call people by their first names. One Sophisticate recalls that he was visited at his office by a cousin who stood nervously fidgeting with his hat and referring to his cousin as 'Sir'. It took the Sophisticate several insistent attempts before he succeeded in making his caller a little less formal. Ironically, denial of the right to deference does not reduce the perceived social distance in such an interaction; it simply embarrasses the 'inferior', making him feel insecure in the relationship and resentful at being thus patronised. To deny the right to deference is also to deny the legitimacy of the relation of inequality. Whilst, in Newfoundland, deference (or, what Perlin (1972) calls 'the "Mr" John phenomenon') is historically the product of subservience, it emerges now as a culturally conditioned response. To deny it is to reject the values on which it is based. And thus in trying to conceal their lack of legitimacy, the Sophisticates actually succeed only in exacerbating it. Their behaviour is interpreted as an assertion of the irrelevance and redundancy of traditional political culture.

RELUCTANCE TO LEAD

Just as deference lends legitimacy to the People's Group, and denies it to the Sophisticates, so also does the reluctance to assume positions of leadership and responsibility. It is a reluctance manifest in diverse areas of social life, extending from the governmental to occupational spheres. Faris (1972) notes a strong equalitarian ethos in Cat Harbour community life which is offended by any attempt to assume a leadership posture. Such repugnant behaviour is regarded as aggression. Nemec (1972b) and Stiles (1972) both find that the decisional structure of the nearshore fishing crew tends to be horizontal rather than hierarchical, and they describe the established procedures by which skippers attempt to neutralise their status differential, and to share their decision-making responsibilities. The skipper's reticence, like the Focaltowner's, may well derive from fear of being made a scapegoat or of being responsible for failure. Among Focaltowners there seems also to be a feeling of inadequacy. Both of these can be understood as results of the structural conditioning referred to above. But the disinclination to lead has become so strongly rooted as to emerge in a suspicion of those who *do* seek leadership roles. Having had a council as early as 1945, and school boards functioning long before that, Focaltowners have come to accept formal or statutory governmental positions of leadership, so long as they are occupied by actors displaying the traditional attributes of leadership—precisely those which characterise the People's Group and the Legitimisers. But leadership through voluntary associations or interest groups, such as the Sophisticates exercise, is treated with extreme suspicion: for if aspiring leadership *generally* invites distrust, leadership which creates the very roles on which it is based, and thus denies the superiority of *legitimate* leadership roles, must be seen as culturally repugnant. The Focaltowner's limited tolerance of leadership extends to that either exercised with reluctance, or based on traditional criteria of ascription or law. He will *submit* to other forms—such as those of the Sophisticates—but will not endow them with legitimacy. His reaction to their exercise is much the same as that of the Cat Harbour people, described by Faris (1972, 103):

Local leadership and the excercise of power are logically viewed as socially aggressive and persons who submit to this behaviour place themselves in potential danger of exploitation.

And, indeed, the imputations of self-interest commonly made to the Sophisticates—who are conscious of them—may be seen to derive from this assumption of exploitation.

I have observed already that in Focaltown, the assumption of a leadership role renders the incumbent vulnerable to attack. It is therefore regarded as a 'foolish' role. Many writers have noted this characteristic in various cultural contexts. If, therefore, people actually aspire to such roles, their motives automatically become suspect; these suspicions are popularly validated by reference to the 'objective' features of the leader's social identity. Thus, traditionally, leaders sought to disguise or to minimise obvious distinguishing characteristics of their superior status. Their homes and dress were unobtrusive, their social interaction was typical of their subjects' in the local community. I have described such presentational strategies as characteristic of the People's Group activists. The Sophisticates, by contrast, display identities which clearly mark them out from their neighbours (see Cohen, 1975*a*), and in so doing they exacerbate the derogatory judgements which are made in respect of their eagerness to take over the community's leadership. Whilst, then, both groups exploit the popular reluctance to lead in order to husband their leadership roles, they are also subject to evaluation by reference to this reluctance. Here, again, the People's Group members benefit from the Sophisticates' liabilities, and they manage their impressions accordingly. Thus, they contrive an appearance of prominent men who recognise a responsibility to provide leadership. They appear to be appropriately reticent about engaging in the business of leadership. In this way they underline the Sophisticates' aggression.

The problem of legitimacy: conclusion 123

Like the cultural characteristic of deference, then, this marked reluctance to lead affects the competing leaders in two ways. It enables them to maintain the vertical political relationship of leaders and led by mitigating popular demands for participation in leadership. But it also provides a set of values employed in the attribution or denial of legitimacy to leaders.

THE ABSENCE OF COLLECTIVE IDENTITY

The same two effects are present in the Focaltowner's disinclination to organise collectively or to identify his interests with those of the wider community.

We noted early in this essay that the establishment of Edward Martin's political dominance in Focaltown was facilitated by the scarcity of willing leaders. The leadership for which Focaltowners look is that which operates within a clearly delineated sphere of authority and does not require of the citizens any communal or co-operative effort. So far as the legitimate institutional positions of authority are concerned, the Focaltowner's attitude is that if there is anyone foolish enough to lead, he'll be led—so long as no sacrifice is demanded of him. He is, by inclination, a subject rather than a participant: he does not have the sense of community (or communality) which is required to effect a transition in this status. Focaltown has no tradition of solidarity, in the organisational and associational senses. Like Cat Harbour, the minimal shared identity which it does have

... is simply a function of common adaptation to given circumstances [Faris, 1972, 106, n. 74].

As one of my Legitimiser informants mildly put it:

... Focaltown is composed of citizens, but frankly I think that, if one is honest about it ... it really consists of individuals. Mr Jones living down the street isn't too worried about Mr Smith who lives next door ... There is a lot of this.

There is, though, something of a myth about Focaltown's communalism, and its currency inhibits its denial. In this sense, the familism or absence of communal identity to which I refer may be regarded as a construct, though again, one for which there is the justification of intuition.

In the 1969 survey respondents were given two hypothetical situations, in the first of which a person's contribution to the community would be to the slight disadvantage of his family—for example, by slightly reducing the time he could spend at home; and in the second, serving his family's interest might have a slightly adverse affect on the community. In each case, the respondent was asked to prescribe the action he thought right. The answers to both questions showed a clear and, perhaps, not very surprising tendency to place the community after the family. But, as a comparison of tables 7 and 8 will show, it was very much more marked in the first question than in the second, a difference which might be explained by the greater personal effort implied in the first and, indeed, by the greater universality of the former example than that in the latter question.

Table 7. Distribution of responses, indicating family and community orientation, to question: 'Suppose a person could do something which would help his community but might harm his family. For example, suppose he volunteered to serve on some organisation which would give him less time at home. Should he do it, or not?'

Response	Herring Bay		Focaltown	
	N	%	N	%
Should do it	35	9·0	3	8·3
Should not do it	329	84·1	31	86·1
Depends	11	2·8	1	2·8
Don't know	16	4·1	1	2·8
Total	391	100·0	36	100·0

Table 8. Distribution of responses, indicating family and community orientation, to question: "Suppose a person could do something which would help his family but might harm his community. For example, he has a piece of land which he wants to use for some purpose but the council also wants it for a community project. Should he act for his own advantage or for the community's advantage?'

Response	Herring Bay		Focaltown	
	N	%	N	%
Own advantage	184	47·1	18	50·0
Community's advantage	148	37·8	16	44·4
Depends	40	10·3	—	—
Don't know	19	4·8	2	5·6
Total	391	100·0	36	100·0

It is against this unpromising background of familism that the Sophisticates seek legitimacy for themselves by managing myths of 'community service'. Quite apart from the rejection of traditional values which is implied by the Sophisticate organisation, the Focaltowner can only make Sophisticate behaviour intelligible to himself by imputing to it familistic or self-interested motives. The Sophisticates' not unnatural response is to insist that whilst their activities may benefit themselves, this consequence is incidental to the benefit which accrues to the community as a whole. There clearly is some truth in this for while, for example, Eaton is accused of self-interest in his relations with the Economic Development Association and the Stadium Commission, Farrar of political ambition in his organisational activity, and all of the Sophisticates except John Whiteway of complicity in 'mismanagement' of school board affairs, their activity in each of these areas does involve the provision of public facilities. Their defence has no salience, however. For, as was long ago noted for Newfoundland society in general (Newfoundland Royal Commission, 1933, 82-3), the provision of public services by a leader has come to be looked upon by the Focaltown public as an obligation rather than as a favour, and the services thus provided have been used simply because they were offered rather than because they satisfied a public need (cf. Evans, n.d., 15). It is a conditioned reflex of a society which has traditionally been articulated through patronage. Whilst they are compliant followers, Focaltowners demand some demonstration of the benefits—in terms of the provision of services—of being led. The leader's performance, in this respect, is not a means by which he may seek support: it is a *prerequisite* of the search for support. It is the means by which he identifies himself as a leader; the search for, and attribution of, support comes later. The Sophisticates' largesse is, therefore, not looked upon as a prestation requiring exchange through support: it is regarded simply as a kind of test of their acuity as leaders. It has nothing to offer them by way of legitimacy; indeed, quite the reverse, for it is invariably the pay-off to the leader rather than the public's benefit which exercises the public imagination. One of the ironies of Focaltown political culture, then, is that it predisposes the individual to satisfy his own interests at the possible expense of others—but makes suspicion of similar behaviour in his leaders grounds for condemnation.

Whilst these related notions of self-interest and deference may thus resemble explanatory constructs, the disinclination to organise is ubiquitously and unmistakably apparent in Focaltown social life. It does not affect merely the overtly political, but is evident everywhere. Faris shows how even so customary a procedure as the annual 'lottery' for trap berths in Cat Harbour becomes a crisis as a consequence of the participant fishermen's inability to organise themselves:

... the annual cod trap berth drawing is ... a long and agonising affair, for hours are spent on decisions about just who is to draw for the crew and what berth the person drawing will choose [1972, 103].

The industrialised occupations of Focaltown clearly require greater coordination than the Cat Harbour fishery, but it does not appear to be much easier to achieve. Woods foremen often complained of the difficulty of establishing integrated and specialised work procedures, and nostalgia for the old days of independence and autonomous activity is frequently expressed by loggers. Labour union activity among miners is minimal, even in one of the local companies whose working conditions and wages are clearly inferior to those elsewhere.

To some extent, of course, this antipathy to organisation can be explained by the atomisim of Focaltown society, discussed above. But it is also a potent resource exploited by politicians who recognise in it a means of maintaining the impotence of the local people and, therefore, of nurturing their own indispensability. Neither group of leaders in Focaltown, therefore, seeks to change the popular attitude to participation; rather, each capitalises on it. But their claims to legitimacy are also evaluated by the public in terms of the repugnance of organisation.

Sophisticate political behaviour imposes leadership through agencies which exclude popular participation. People's Group behaviour conforms with traditional values by making organisation and participation 'unnecessary'. Stan Lester's brokerage activity is symptomatic of the disinclination of outport populations to organise. Firstly, the communities look for a broker because they do not have the organisational structure on which to base their own demands. Secondly, they seek, through the broker, short-term aid for the alleviation of immediate problems (cf. Evans, n.d.); so long as these customary forms of patronage were available, there was no constraint on them to establish organisational structures for the long-term planning which might obviate the necessity of seeking the short-term palliative.

There is, then, a cultural sanction which is applied to organisation. It is an obstacle which the groups have to negotiate in order both to sustain their leadership, and to acquire legitimacy. The culture-extending strategy logically prescribes that the extent to which contemporary leadership requires organisational involvement should be minimised or, at least, obscured from public view. Cultural substitution, on the other hand, proclaims the intrinsic value of organisational endeavour and, by implication, the redundancy of the traditional anti-organisational value. These strategic imperatives explain the groups' contrasting approaches to the town council, which is interesting as the only Focaltown organisation, apart from the school boards, which requires direct public compliance, through the payment of tax.

Whilst People's Group members do belong to community organisations, they are neither active in nor identified with them—with the exception of the 'legitimate' institution of the town council. The Sophisticate elite, as political entrepreneurs, deny the salience of council, both as an institution *per se*, and as usually constituted. Local government law in Newfoundland is such as to discourage policy formulation and initiation. Councils are required to obtain approval from the government for all expenditures: in the absence of such approval, councillors who voted for the expenditure become personally liable for any loss incurred. The Provincial Department of Municipal Affairs thus retains effective control of the councils (cf. Crosbie, 1956, especially 342). Further, a frequent Sophisticate complaint is that not only has the council not raised the taxes, but it does not even collect them efficiently. The council did once half-heartedly consider raising the tax rate, but was intimidated into dropping the matter when its meeting was interrupted by the noisy arrival of several highly inebriated citizens—all of whom were already in debt to the council—demanding that the issue be 'shelved' in perpetuity. One of the Legitimisers, who was a councillor at the time, describes council's reaction:

... it really shook the council, you know; it was quite a bad night for us. But we decided that rather than force the issue and really put ourselves into hot water, we'd better just let them do without the things that should be done and get along the best way we could without the increase in taxes ...

As one might expect, the Sophisticates, who assert their right to make and implement policy in the community, had no sympathy with the councillors. Moreover, their success in mobilising independent resources would deny any value to their participation in an organisation which is forcibly submitted to government direction and which is little more than an administrative extension of the Department of Municipal Affairs. There is one Sophisticate on council—Ivan Lush—who seems to have sought election in pursuit of his amibition to become mayor and, perhaps, to enhance his claim to the Progressive Conservative candidacy for Herring Bay.

We can conclude that the People's Group's involvement in the town council does not infringe the community's anti-organisation ethic and, indeed, the activists are careful not to push council policy—as on taxation—to the point at which it might offend the public's sensibilities. The Sophisticates, however, condemn council precisely because it does not contravene popular values, and then indulge in organisational activity which does not require any public participation or compliance. Both strategies therefore protect the leadership roles from public incursion, but they are not equally successful in winning legitimacy.

This absence of collective identity, and the associated disinclination to organise are, with deference and the reluctance to lead, impediments to the development of new forms of leadership which might dislodge those practised and husbanded by the People's Group and the Sophisticates. Their control of the level of leadership is not in jeopardy, but their legitimacy is very much in question. The antagonistic myth-managing strategies of cultural extension and cultural substitution, whose ramifications have been reviewed in these chapters, are called for precisely by the need to resolve this crisis of legitimacy.

Early in this book I argued against the view that power is, by definition, legitimate, suggesting instead that power provides access to legitimacy and that, in turn, legitimacy can be used to enhance and increase power. The two entities are conceptually distinct but empirically they may stand in a reciprocal relation, the one reinforcing the other. Both the People's

Group and the Sophisticates have 'power'—in the minimal sense we have abstracted from the various usages of the word: in certain situations, they can get what they want to get, and can do what they want to do. We have seen also that by virtue of their traditionalism and association with the legitimating values of custom, the People's Group is legitimated to a greater degree than are their rivals. Does this mean that they are more powerful? The answer, I think, is no. Apart from suggesting the frailty of those organisational values implicit in their myths of legitimisation, the very fact that they are constantly required to renew their legitimacy indicates that the People's Group activists have departed in various respects from the traditional legitimated norm. Cultural extension is the attempt to bridge the gap between this hallowed tradition and the contemporary structural situation. We have seen that it is the struggle for legitimacy which pushes the activists into their culture-extending stances. They are postures which can only be maintained within their existing leadership positions: that is to say, their legitimacy is threatened by any attempt they make to increase their power. To put it the other way around, they cannot increase the extent to which they impinge themselves upon the community without jeopardising their legitimacy. The two significant points here are, firstly, that the means by which they have traditionally sustained themselves—patronage—are decreasingly available and appropriate; secondly, their greater legitimacy is the only resource on which their superiority over the Sophisticates is based. If it goes, so then does this superiority, for they would then be forced back on to the kinds of leadership which the Sophisticates exercise with much greater skill. So far, then, as the People's Group is concerned, legitimacy is becoming the sole means by which its leadership status can be maintained.

For the Sophisticates the situation is, in some respects, the reverse, for they, again, have roles in which leadership can be exercised, but they have no legitimacy. Unlike the People's Group, their leadership roles are not currently contingent on legitimacy for, in the short run, they are based on the independent resources given by their organisational activities and entrepreneurial skills. Theirs is an imposed rather than a supported style of leadership, but one which can be effectively limited by the lack of legitimacy, as we saw in the case of the Economic Development Association. Imposed structures, of course, never remain 'pure' for long. If they can survive for long enough, they tend to be mediated by the cultural contexts in which they operate—which they also change. But in order to maintain their own incumbency of the leadership roles they have created, the Sophisticates have to ensure that they remain strategically placed to manage the myths on which the organisations are based; that is, they have to maintain these structures in an unmediated form until the myths are sufficiently well-established to bear the distortion which would follow from their incorporation into indigenous cultural experience. Clearly, one means which is available to them in this regard is to create dependency upon their own leadership, and to do this they must discredit the People's Group by showing its leadership to be based on outmoded values and to have been rendered redundant by political and economic change. Sophisticate mythology has to be depicted as more appropriate to contemporary exigencies than the myths of cultural extension. Thus, the Sophisticates' struggle for legitimacy is, also, directly a struggle to deprive the People's Group of its legitimacy.

What is clearly at issue between the groups, then, is not positions of power, or valued roles: it is those very values which sustain leadership. What is at issue is legitimacy itself. It is in that sense that legitimacy constitutes an unequally distributed resource which structures the political relation between the two groups. It is what the politics of Focaltown's leadership is all about.

THE POLITICS OF LEGITIMACY AND THE POLITICS OF EVERYDAY LIFE[3]

This book has been concerned with the ways in which activists in a community's leadership respond to what they perceive as a crisis of political legitimacy. It began with the suggestion that politics should be seen as a feature of everyday social life, rather than as an institutionally or functionally discrete activity. In this regard, the politics of legitimacy may be seen as a ubiquitous dimension of social interaction, being akin also to the common problems with which people contend in their social presentation of identity. It has been argued that the struggle for identity is tantamount to a search for the social confirmation of self (Klapp, 1969); the struggle for legitimisation by the Focaltown leaders might well be regarded as a search for the social confirmation of political self.

But the pursuits of legitimacy and of valued identity are alike in other respects as well—theoretically and substantively. They are, firstly, both *strategic* activities. The two styles of myth management, for example, called into being by the trauma of socio-cultural change, have their counterparts in the presentation of identities which have been thrown into crisis by social circumstances. Various studies have shown that actors whose identities have become stigmatised in one way or another respond by strategically over-communicating or under-communicating the stigmatic components of their identities (see Goffman, 1968; Eidheim, 1969; Berreman, 1973; Glass, 1962; Habenstein, 1962). The first 'assertive' strategy would advertise as positive values those elements of identity which others have stigmatised, through slogans ('Black is Beautiful'), fashion, speech, co-residence or 'ghettorisation' (Wadel, 1973, 92–3), or simply by a resolute adherence to customary values. The alternative 'assimilative' mode of identity management seeks to obscure the stigma by adopting the appurtenances of identity of the 'normals'—those who impose the stigmatic label. Common to both strategies is a procedure of 'introverted stigmatisation', in which stigmatised groups turn inwards to develop their own categories of centrality and peripherality, normality and stigmatisation.

There is a sense in which outport Newfoundlanders have, following Confederation, been labouring under a stigma—of marginality—implicit in the Province's image in the rest of Canada. The marginality of the outports has been further underlined by the decline in traditional subsistence activities, the large-scale relocation and centralisation of the outport population, and by the government's emphasis on industrialisation. The various modes of stigma control appear as ubiquitous tendencies in Focaltown's social life and, indeed, coincide with the dichotomous strategies of myth management. Thus assertive marginality is associated strategically with cultural extension, whilst 'assimilation', the adoption of metropolitan political and social life-styles is implicit in cultural substitution.

But these associations extend beyond the level of leadership, and underpin the dualism within the community as a whole which sustains the leadership conflict. Thus, they tend to coincide with divisions among the town's population between sects; between the employed and upwardly mobile, and the unemployed and non-mobile; between 'insiders' and 'outsiders'. But, above all, they reflect an ideological division—between the 'ordinary' (assertive marginality) and the 'extraordinary' (assimilative marginality)—which might be typical of societies traditionally habituated to subsistence living and suddenly faced with an explosion of materialism. 'Ordinariness' was locally expressed in the epithet of 'the good man', applied to those who manifested the diffuse criterial values on which status was based in traditional community life—neighbourliness; providing well for one's family; being honest and hard-working; possessing traditional skills or being fairly self-sufficient in such matters as building a house, gathering fuel, fishing and hunting; reticence; and displaying awareness of one's place in the world by deferring to authority and those in (legitimately) superior positions. It was precisely the hitherto unquestioned integrity of this identity which was challenged by the materialistic ethic which underpinned the rise of the new middle class, and which was expressed in the culturally-alien values which informed the presentational styles of the Sophisticates. Those fundamental values in accordance with which identity had previously been organised were no longer being taken for granted. Now their integrity had to be reaffirmed through their competitive juxtaposition with new values and identities. Worse, not only had they to confront differing values, but they were also repugned by them.

The concerns of the activists with their legitimacy as leaders was thus complemented by a general concern with the definition of legitimate and valued social identities, both rendered problematic by the processes of quite fundamental socio-cultural change in which rural Newfoundland is immersed. For the ordinary, non-activist, Focaltowner, the resources acquired by the successful presentation of a salient and valued identity are no less useful in his interactional strategies than is legitimacy to the leaders. Both thus have *political* dimensions, in the sense in which 'politics' has been used in this book, and it is in precisely this regard that one speaks of 'politics' as being an element of everyday life. The public behaviour of leaders seeking support is different only in degree—but not in kind—and thus provides us with an illustrative model of processes common in everyday social interaction.

NOTES TO CHAPTER SEVEN

[1] It should be borne in mind that the vast majority of these communities are exclusively Protestant. In the Catholic outports of Newfoundland the priest was invariably an extremely powerful man (see Nemec, 1972a). In Focaltown the Protestant clergy were not regarded as holding power in the secular world and, indeed, sought only a minimal involvement in those community activities which were not held under the aegis of the Churches.

[2] For vivid descriptions of the early systems of legal repression in Newfoundland, see McLintock (1941). Also Prowse (1895).

[3] The following section is amplified ethnographically in Cohen (1975a).

Bibliography

BOOKS AND ARTICLES

Apter, David (1963), 'Political religion in the new nations', in *Old Societies and New States: the Quest for Modernity in Asia and Africa*, edited by C. Geertz, pp. 57-104. New York: Free Press of Glencoe.

Asad, Talal (1970), *The Kababish Arabs: Power, Authority and Consent in a Nomadic Tribe*. London: G. Hurst & Co.

Bachrach, P., and Baratz, H. (1962), 'Two faces of power', *American Political Science Review*, vol. 56 (4), pp. 947-52.

Bailey, F. G. (1968), 'Parapolitical systems', in *Local-level Politics: Social and Cultural Perspectives*, edited by M. Swartz, pp. 281-94. Chicago: Aldine Publishing Co.

—— (1969), *Stratagems and Spoils: a Social Anthropology of Politics*. Oxford: Basil Blackwell.

—— (1971), 'The peasant view of the bad life', in *Peasants and Peasant Societies: Selected Readings*, edited by T. Shanin, pp. 299-321. Harmondsworth: Penguin Books.

Balandier, G (1970), *Political Anthropology* (trans. A M. Sheridan-Smith). London: Allen Lane, The Penguin Press.

Banfield, E. C. (1958), *The Moral Basis of a Backward Society*. New York: Free Press of Glencoe.

Barnes, J. A. (1969), 'Networks and political process', in *Social Networks in Urban Situations: Analyses of Personal Relationships in Central African Towns*, edited by J. C. Mitchell, pp. 51-76. Manchester: Manchester University Press for the Institute for African Studies.

Barth, Fredrik (1963), Introduction to *The Role of the Entrepreneur in Social Change in Northern Norway*, edited by F. Barth, pp. 5-18. Bergen: Norwegian Universities Press.

—— (1965), *Political Leadership Among Swat Pathans*. London: Athlone Press.

—— (1966), *Models of Social Organisation*, Royal Anthropological

Institute Occasional Paper 23. London: Royal Anthropological Institute.

Berreman, G. D. (1973), 'Self, situation, and escape from stigmatised ethnic identity', in *Management of Minority Status*, edited by J. Brøgger, pp. 11–25. Oslo: Universitetsforlaget.

Bienen, H. (1970), *Tanzania: Party Transformation and Economic Development*. Princeton: Princeton University Press.

Blau, P. (1964), *Exchange and Power in Social Life*, New York: John Wiley.

Boissevain, J. (1966), 'Patronage in Sicily', *Man*, n.s., vol. 1 (1), pp. 18–33.

—— (1974), *Friends of Friends: Networks, Manipulators and Coalitions*. Oxford: Basil Blackwell.

Brox, O. (1972), *Newfoundland Fishermen in an Age of Industry: a Sociology of Economic Dualism*, Newfoundland Social and Economic Studies, 9, second edition. St John's: Institute of Social & Economic Research, Memorial University of Newfoundland.

Catton, W. (1966), *From Animistic to Naturalistic Sociology*. New York: McGraw-Hill.

Cicourel, A. V. (1964), *Method and Measurement in Sociology*. New York: Free Press of Glencoe.

Cohen, A. (1969), 'Political Anthropology: the Analysis of the Symbolism of Power Relations', *Man*, n.s., vol. 4 (2), pp. 215–35.

Cohen, A. P. (1975a), 'The definition of public identity: managing marginality in outport Newfoundland following Confederation', *Sociological Review*, Vol. 23 (1), February.

—— (1975b), 'The political context of childhood: leaders and anti-leaders in a changing Newfoundland community,' in *Socialisation and Values in Contemporary Canada*, edited by R. M. Pike and E. Zureik. Toronto: Carleton Library.

Cohen, A. P. and Comaroff, J. L. (forthcoming), 'The management of meaning: on the phenomenology of political transactions', in ASA monograph series *New Directions in Social Anthropology*, volume on transactional theory, edited by B. Kapferer. London: Jossey-Bass.

Cohen, D. L. (1972), 'The concept of charisma and the analysis of leadership', in *Political Studies*, vol. 20 (3), pp. 299–305.

Cohen, P. S. (1969), 'Theories of myth', *Man*, n.s., vol. 4 (3), pp. 337–53.

Copes, P. (1970), *Fishermen's Vote in Newfoundland*, discussion paper 70-1-1, Department of Economics and Commerce, Simon Fraser University, Burnaby.

Costa Pinto, L. A. (1965), 'Portrait of developing man: the processes of social changes in Latin America', in *The New Sociology: Essays in Social Science and Social Theory in Honour of C. Wright Mills*, edited by I. L. Horowitz, pp. 464–75. New York: Oxford University Press.

Crosbie, J. C. (1956), 'Local government in Newfoundland', *Canadian Journal of Economics and Political Science*, vol. 22 (3), pp. 332–46.

Crysdale, S. (1965), *The Changing Church in Canada: Beliefs and Social Attitudes of United Church People*. Toronto: Board of Evangelicalism and Social Service, United Church of Canada.

Dahrendorf, R. (1958), 'Out of Utopia: toward a reorientation of sociological analysis', *American Journal of Sociology*, vol. 64 (2), pp. 115-27.

Danzger, M. H. (1964), 'Community power structure: problems and continuities', *American Sociological Review*, vol. 29 (5), pp. 707-17.

Devons, Ely (1956), 'The role of the myth in politics', *The Listener*, 21 June, pp. 843-4.

DeWitt, R. L. (1969), *Public Policy and Community Protest: the Fogo Case*, Newfoundland Social and Economic Studies, 8. St John's: Institute of Social & Economic Research, Memorial University of Newfoundland.

Dore, R. F. (1971), 'Modern co-operation in traditional communities', in *Two Blades of Grass: Rural Co-operatives in Agricultural Modernisation* edited by P. M. Worsley, pp. 43-60. Manchester: Manchester University Press.

Douglas, M. (1966), *Purity and Danger: an Analysis of Concepts of Pollution and Taboo*. London: Routledge & Kegan Paul.

Easton, D. (1957), 'An approach to the analysis of political systems', *World Politics*, vol. 9 (3), pp. 383-400.

— (1959), 'Political anthropology', in *The Biennial Review of Anthropology, 1959*, edited by B. J. Siegel, pp. 210-62. Stanford: Stanford University Press.

— (1965a), *A Framework for Political Analysis*. Englewood Cliffs, N.J.: Prentice-Hall.

— (1965b), *A Systems Analysis of Political Life*. New York: John Wiley.

— (1966), 'Alternative strategies in theoretical research', in *Varieties of Political Theory*, pp. 1-13. Englewood Cliffs, N.J.: Prentice-Hall.

Edelman, M. (1964), *The Symbolic Uses of Politics*. Urbana: University of Illinois Press.

Eidheim, H. (1969), 'When ethnic identity is a social stigma', in *Ethnic Groups and Boundaries: the Social Organisation of Culture Difference*, edited by F. Barth. London: Allen & Unwin.

Epstein, A. L. (1968), 'Power, politics and leadership: some Central African and Melanesian contrasts', in *Local-level Politics: Social and Cultural Perspectives*, edited by M. Swartz, pp. 53-68. Chicago: Aldine Publishing Co.

Evans, F. J. (1966), 'The challenge and conflict of change: a social and economic report on rural Newfoundland', St John's: mimeo.

— (n.d.), 'Social animation', St John's: mimeo.

Evans-Pritchard, E. E. (1940), *The Nuer*. Oxford: Clarendon Press.

Fallers, L. A. (1963), 'Political sociology and the study of African politics', *European Journal of Sociology*, vol. 4, pp. 311-29.

Faris, J. C. (1972), *Cat Harbour: a Newfoundland Fishing Settlement*, Newfoundland Social & Economic Studies, 3, second edition. St John's: Institute of Social and Economic Research, Memorial University of Newfoundland.

Feltham, J. (1959), 'The development of the F.P.U. in Newfoundland, 1908-23', unpublished M.A. thesis, Memorial University of Newfoundland.

Fortes, M. and Evans-Pritchard, E. E. (1940), Introduction to *African Political Systems*, pp. 1-23. London: Oxford University Press for the International African Institute.

Foster, G. (1962), *Traditional Cultures and the Impact of Technological Change*. New York: Harper & Row.

—— (1963), 'The dyadic contract in Tzintzuntzan: patron-client relationship', *American Anthropologist*, vol. 63 (6).

Frankenberg, R. (1957), *Village on the Border*. London: Cohen & West.

Freeman, M. M. R. (ed.) (1969), *Intermediate Adaptation in Newfoundland and the Arctic: a Strategy of Social and Economic Development*, Newfoundland Social and Economic Papers, 4. St John's: Institute of Social & Economic Research, Memorial University of Newfoundland.

Glaser, B. G. and Strauss, A. L. (1967), *The Discovery of Grounded Theory: Strategies for Qualitative Research*. Chicago: Aldine Publishing Co.

Glass, R. (1962), 'Insiders-outsiders: the position of minorities', *New Left Review*, vol. 17, winter, pp. 34-45.

Glickman, H. (1965), 'One-party system in Tanzania', *Annals of the American Academy of Political and Social Science*, vol. 358, pp. 136-49.

—— (1967), 'Dilemmas of political theory in an African context: the ideology of Julius Nyerere', in *Boston University Papers on Africa*, edited by J. Butler and A. Castagno, pp. 195-223. New York: Praeger.

Gluckman, H. Max (1962), 'Les Rites de passage', in *Essays on the Ritual of Social Relations*, pp. 1-52. Manchester: Manchester University Press.

—— (1965), *Politics, Law and Ritual in Tribal Society*. Oxford: Basil Blackwell.

Goffman, E. (1968), *Stigma: Notes on the Management of Spoiled Identity*. Harmondsworth: Penguin Books.

—— (1971), *Relations in Public: Microstudies of the Public Order*. London: Allen Lane, The Penguin Press.

—— (1972), *Interaction Ritual: Essays on Face-to-face Behaviour*. London: Allen Lane, The Penguin Press.

Goody, J. (1961), 'Religion and ritual: the definitional problem', *British Journal of Sociology*, vol. 12 (2), pp. 142-64.

Gouldner, A. (1960), 'The norm of reciprocity: a preliminary statement', *American Sociological Review*, vol. 25 (2), pp. 161-78.

Gwyn, R. (1968), *Smallwood: the Unlikely Revolutionary*. Toronto: McClelland & Stewart.

Habenstein, R. W. (1962), 'Sociology of occupations: the case of the American funeral director', in *Human Behaviour and Social Processes: an Interactionist Approach*, edited by A. M. Rose, pp. 225-46. London: Routledge & Kegan Paul.

Harris, L. (1969), 'Newfoundland and Confederation, 1948-9', in *Regionalism in the Canadian Community, 1867-1967*, edited by M. Wade, pp. 227-63. Toronto: University of Toronto Press.

Herrick, C. S. (1968), 'Regional development and the Atlantic region: a look at some alternatives', *Proceedings of the tenth Annual Meeting of the Western Association of Sociology & Anthropology*, Banff.

Historical Statistics of Newfoundland and Labrador, (1970), St John's: Government of Newfoundland and Labrador.

Hodgkin, T. (1964), 'The relevance of "Western" ideas for the new African States', in *Self-government in Modernising Nations*, edited by J. R. Pennock, pp. 50-80. Englewood Cliffs, N.J.: Prentice-Hall.

Homans, G. C. (1951), *The Human Group*. London: Routledge & Kegan Paul.

—— (1971), 'Bringing men back in', in *Institutions and Social Exchange: the Sociologies of Talcott Parsons and George C. Homans*, edited by H. Turk and R. L. Simpson, pp. 102-16. Indianapolis: Bobbs-Merrill Co.

Horwood, H. (1967), *Tomorrow will be Sunday*. Toronto: McClelland & Stewart.

—— (1969), 'Newfoundland and Confederation, 1948-9', in *Regionalism in the Canadian Community, 1867-1967*, edited by M. Wade, pp. 227-63. Toronto: University of Toronto Press.

Hoselitz, B. F. (1961), 'Tradition and economic growth', in *Tradition, Values and Socio-economic Development*, edited by R. Braibanti and J. J. Spengler, pp. 83-113. Durham, N.C.: Duke University Press.

Iverson, N. and Matthews, D. R. (1968), *Communities in Decline: an Examination of Household Resettlement in Newfoundland*, Newfoundland Social and Economic Studies, 6. St. John's: Institute of Social & Economic Research, Memorial University of Newfoundland.

Jacob, P. E. and Teune, H. (1964), 'The integrative process: guidelines for the analysis of the basis of political community', in *The Integration of Political Communities*, edited by P. E. Jacob and J. V. Toscano, pp. 1-45. Philadelphia: J. P. Lippincott Co.

Kavadias, G. (1966), 'The assimilation of the scientific and technological "Message"', *International Social Science Journal*, vol. 18 (3), pp. 362-75.

Kavanagh, D. (1971), 'The deferential English: a comparative critique', *Government and Opposition*, vol 6 (3), pp. 333-60.

Kirk, G. S. (1970), *Myth: its Meaning and Functions in Ancient and Other Cultures*. Cambridge: Cambridge University Press.

Klapp, O. E. (1969), *Collective Search for Identity*. New York: Holt Rinehart and Winston.

Kuper, A. (1970), *Kalahari Village Politics: an African Democracy*. Cambridge: Cambridge University Press.
Laponce, J. A. (1969), 'Canadian party labels: an essay in semantics and anthropology', *Canadian Journal of Political Science*, vol. 2 (2), pp. 141–57.
Leach, E. R. (1966), 'The legitimacy of Solomon', *European Journal of Sociology*, vol. 7, pp. 58–101.
—— (1968), Introduction to *The Structural Study of Myth and Totemism*, ASA monograph 5, pp. vii–xix. London: Tavistock.
—— (1970), *Political Systems of Highland Burma*. London: Athlone Press.
Levine, R. A. (1960), 'The internalisation of political values in Stateless societies', *Human Organisation*, vol. 19 (2), pp. 51–8.
Lévi-Strauss, C. (1965), 'The structural study of myth', in *Myth: a Symposium*, edited by T. Sebeok, pp. 81–106. Bloomington: Indiana University Press.
—— (1966), *The Savage Mind*. Chicago: University of Chicago Press.
Lienhardt, G. (1961), *Divinity and Experience: the Religion of the Dinka*. Oxford: Clarendon Press.
Lodge, T. (1939), *Dictatorship in Newfoundland*. London: Cassell & Co.
McLintock, A. H. (1941), *The Establishment of Constitutional Government in Newfoundland, 1783–1832: a Study of Retarded Colonisation*. London: Longmans Green & Co.
Malinowski, B. (1928), 'The life of myth', *The Saturday Review of Literature*, vol. 4 (37), pp. 738–9.
—— (1963a), 'Myth as a dramatic development of dogma', in *Sex, Culture and Myth*, pp. 245–55. London: Rupert Hart-Davis.
—— (1963b), 'The foundations of faith and morals', in *Sex, Culture and Myth*, pp. 295–336. London: Rupert Hart-Davis.
Maranda, P. (1972), Introduction to *Mythology*, pp. 7–20. Harmondsworth: Penguin Books.
March, J. (1966), 'The power of power', in *Varieties of Political Theory*, edited by D. Easton, pp. 39–70. Englewood Cliffs, N.J.: Prentice-Hall.
Marriott, M. (1963), 'Cultural policy in the new States', in *Old Societies and New States: the Quest for Modernity in Asia and Africa*, edited by C. Geertz, pp. 27–56. New York: The Free Press of Glencoe.
Matthews, D. R. (1970), 'Communities in transition: an examination of government-initiated community migration in rural Newfoundland', unpublished Ph.D. dissertation, University of Minnesota.
Mayer, A. C. (1967), 'Patrons and brokers: rural leadership in four overseas Indian communities', in *Social Organisation: Essays presented to Raymond Firth*, edited by M. Freedman, pp. 167–88. London: Frank Cass.
Miller, J. D. B. (1962), *The Nature of Politics*. London: Duckworth & Co.
Mitchell, W. (1967), *Sociological Analysis and Politics: the Theories of Talcott Parsons*. Englewood Cliffs, N.J.: Prentice-Hall.

Murphy, R. F. (1972), *The Dialectics of Social Life*. London: Allen & Unwin.
Nadel, S. F. (1951), *The Foundations of Social Anthropology*. London: Cohen & West.
—— (1954), *Nupe Religion*. London: Routledge & Kegan Paul.
Nemec, T. F. (1972a), 'Political patronage and brokerage among the Newfoundland Irish', in the seminar, 'Local-level politics in Newfoundland'. St John's: Institute of Social & Economic Research, Memorial University of Newfoundland, mimeo.
—— (1972b), 'I fish with my brother: the structure and behaviour of agnatic-based fishing crews in a Newfoundland Irish outport', in *North Atlantic Fishermen: Anthropological Essays on Modern Fishing*, edited by R. R. Andersen and C. Wadel, Newfoundland Social and Economic Papers, 5, pp. 9–34. St John's: Institute of Social & Economic Research, Memorial University of Newfoundland.
Nettler, Gwynn (1970), *Explanations*. New York: McGraw-Hill.
Newfoundland Royal Commission (1933), *Report of the Newfoundland Royal Commission*, Cmd. 4480. London: H.M.S.O.
Noel, S. J. R. (1971), *Politics in Newfoundland*. Toronto: University of Toronto Press.
Nyerere, J. (1962), *Ujamaa: the Basis of African Socialism*. Dar es Salaam: Tanganyika Standard.
Paine, R. P. B. (1971), 'A theory of patronage and brokerage', in *Patrons and Brokers in the East Arctic*, Newfoundland Social and Economic Papers, 2, pp. 8–21. St John's: Institute of Social & Economic Research, Memorial University of Newfoundland.
—— (1973), 'Transactions as communicative events, presented to the decennial meeting of the Association of Social Anthropologists', *New Directions in Social Anthropology*, Oxford.
Parsons, T. (1960), 'Authority, legitimation and political action', in *Structure and Process in Modern Societies*, pp. 170–98. New York: Free Press of Glencoe.
—— (1966a), 'On the concept of political power', in *Class, Status and Power: social stratification in comparative perspective*, edited by R. Bendix and S. M. Lipset, second edition, pp. 240–65. New York: Free Press of Glencoe.
—— (1966b), 'The political aspect of social structure and process', in *Varieties of Political Theory*, edited by D. Easton, pp. 72–112. Englewood Cliffs, N.J.: Prentice-Hall.
—— (1969), 'Polity and society: some general considerations', in *Politics and Social Structure*, pp. 473–522. New York: Free Press of Glencoe.
Perlin, A. B. (1959), *The Story of Newfoundland*. St John's: Guardian Publishing.
Perlin, G. C. (1968), 'The constitutional referendum of 1948 and the revival of sectarianism in Newfoundland politics', *Queen's Quarterly*, vol. 75 (1).

—— (1971), 'Patronage and paternalism: politics in Newfoundland', in *Social Space: Canadian Perspectives*, edited by D. I. Davies and K. Herman. Toronto: New Press.

—— (1972), 'Social change, the mobilization of electoral support and political development in Newfoundland', in the seminar, 'Local-level politics in Newfoundland'. St John's: Institute of Social & Economic Research, Memorial University of Newfoundland, mimeo.

Prowse, D. W. (1895), *A History of Newfoundland from the English, Colonial and Foreign Records*. London: Macmillan & Co.

Radcliffe-Brown, A. R. (1940), Preface to *African Political Systems*, edited by M. Fortes and E. E. Evans-Pritchard, pp. xi–xxiii. London: Oxford University Press for the International African Institute.

—— (1952), *Structure and Function in Primitive Society: Essays and Addresses*. London: Cohen & West.

Royal Commission on the Economic State and Prospects of Newfoundland (1968). St John's: Government of Newfoundland and Labrador.

Rowe, F. W. (1952), *The History of Education in Newfoundland*. Toronto: Ryerson Press.

Sharrock, W. W. (1970), 'The problem of order', in *Introducing Sociology*, edited by P. M. Worsley, pp. 337–92. Harmondsworth: Penguin Books.

Silverman, S. F. (1965), 'Patronage and community–nation relationships in central Italy', *Ethnology*, vol. 4 (2), pp. 172–89.

Skolnik, M. (ed.) (1968), *Viewpoints on Communities in Crisis*, Newfoundland Social and Economic Papers, 1. St John's: Institute of Social & Economic Research, Memorial University of Newfoundland.

Smallwood, J. R. (1927), *Coaker of Newfoundland*. London: Labour Publishing Co.

—— (1973), *I Chose Canada: the Memoirs of the Hon. Joseph R. 'Joey' Smallwood*. Toronto: Macmillan.

Smith, Marjorie (1968), 'Newfoundland, 1815–40: a study of a merchantocracy', unpublished M.A. thesis, Memorial University of Newfoundland.

Smith, M. G. (1956), 'On segmentary lineage systems,' *Journal of the Royal Anthropological Institute*, vol. 86 (II), pp. 39–80.

—— (1960), *Government in Zazzau, 1800–1950*. London: Oxford University Press for the International African Institute.

Sperber, D. (1967), 'Edmund Leach et les anthropologues', *Cahiers Internationaux de Sociologie*, vol. 43, pp. 123–42.

Stiles, R. G. (1971), 'Committees, politics and leaders: some reflections on the heterogeneity of the Newfoundland outport', in 'The colloquium on community aspects of political development'. St John's: Institute of Social & Economic Research Memorial University of Newfoundland, mimeo.

— (1972), 'Fishermen, wives and radios: aspects of communication in a Newfoundland fishing community', in *North Atlantic Fishermen: Anthropological Essays on Modern Fishing*, edited by R. R. Andersen and C. Wadel, Newfoundland Social and Economic Papers, 5, pp. 35–60. St John's: Institute of Social & Economic Research, Memorial University of Newfoundland.

Swartz, M. (1968), Introduction to *Local-level Politics: Social and Cultural Perspectives*, pp. 1–46. Chicago: Aldine Publishing Co.

Swartz, M., Turner, V. W., and Tuden, A. (eds.) (1966), *Political Anthropology*. Chicago: Aldine Publishing Co.

Szwed, J. (1966), *Private Cultures and Public Imagery: Interpersonal Relations in a Newfoundland Peasant Society*, Newfoundland Social and Economic Studies, 2. St John's: Institute of Social & Economic Research, Memorial University of Newfoundland.

Thoms, J. R. (1969), 'A tribute to Joey and Newfoundland's twenty years of Confederation', *Atlantic Advocate*, April, pp. 14–20.

Turner, V. W. (1957), *Schism and Continuity in an African Society*. Manchester: Manchester University Press for the Rhodes-Livingstone Institute.

— (1966), 'Ritual aspects of conflict control in African micropolitics', in *Political Anthropology*, edited by M. Swartz, V. W. Turner, and A. Tuden, pp. 239–46. Chicago: Aldine Publishing Co.

— (1967), *The Forest of Symbols: Aspects of Ndembu Ritual*. Ithaca: Cornell University Press.

— (1969), *The Ritual Process: Structure and Anti-structure*. London: Routledge & Kegan Paul.

Wadel, C. (1969), *Marginal Adaptations and Modernization in Newfoundland: a Study of Strategies and Implications in the Resettlement and Redevelopment of Outport Fishing Communities*, Newfoundland Social and Economic Studies, 7. St John's: Institute of Social & Economic Research, Memorial University of Newfoundland.

— (1969b), 'Public welfare in Newfoundland', paper presented to the annual meeting of the American Anthropological Association, New Orleans.

— (1971), 'Communities and committees: community development and the enlargement of the sense of community on Fogo Island, Newfoundland', in 'The colloquium on community aspects of political development'. St John's: Institute of Social & Economic Research, Memorial University of Newfoundland, mimeo.

— (1973), *Now, whose fault is that? The Struggle for Self-esteem in the Face of Chronic Unemployment*, Newfoundland Social and Economic Studies, 11. St John's: Institute of Social & Economic Research, Memorial University of Newfoundland.

Wagner, G. (1940), 'The political organisation of the Bantu of Kavirondo', in *African Political Systems*, edited by M. Fortes and E. E. Evans-Pritchard, pp. 197–236. London: Oxford University Press for the International African Institute.

White, D. M. (1972), 'The problem of power', *British Journal of Political Science*, vol. 2 (4), pp. 479–90.

Who's Who in Newfoundland and Labrador (1967). St John's.

Willener, A. (1970), *The Action-image of Society: on Cultural Politicisation*, translated by A. M. Sheridan-Smith. London: Tavistock.

Wilson, B. R. (1967), 'The Pentecostalist minister: role conflicts and contradictions of status', in *Patterns of Sectarianism: Organisation and Ideology in Social and Religious Movements*, pp. 138–57. London: Heinemann.

Wolf, E. R. (1966), 'Kinship, friendship and patron–client relations in complex societies', in *The Social Anthropology of Complex Societies*, edited by M. Banton, ASA monograph 4, pp. 1–22. London: Tavistock.

Worsley, P. M. (1964), 'The distribution of power in industrial society', in *The Development of Industrial Societies*, edited by P. Halmos, Sociological Review monograph, 8, pp. 15–34. Keele: University of Keele.

—— (1967), *The Third World*, second edition. London: Weidenfeld & Nicolson.

—— (1970a), 'The concept of populism', in *Populism: its Meanings and National Characteristics*, edited by G. Ionescu and E. Gellner, pp. 212–50. London: Weidenfeld & Nicolson.

—— (1970b), *The Trumpet Shall Sound: a Study of 'Cargo' Cults in Melanesia*, second edition. London: Paladin Books.

—— (1973), 'The revolutionary party as an agency of social change; or, The Politics of Mah-jong', in *Social Science and the New Societies: Problems in Cross-cultural Research and Theory Building*, edited by N. Hammond, pp. 217–45. East Lansing: Social Science Research Bureau, Michigan State University.

NEWSPAPERS

The Daily News, St John's, Newfoundland.
Focaltown News, Focaltown, Newfoundland.
Nearby Town Journal, Nearby Town, Newfoundland.
The Guardian, Manchester and London.
The Loyal Liberal, St John's, Newfoundland.
Newfoundland Bulletin, St John's, Newfoundland.
The Western Star, Cornerbrook, Newfoundland.

Index

'African Socialism', *see under* Nyerere, J.
Alexander, D., 74 n. 12
Anglo-Newfoundland Development Company, 34, 40, 53
Apter, D., 17
Asad, T., 8, 9
Atlantic Provinces Economic Council, 56

Bachrach, P. and Baratz, H., 20 n. 15
Bailey, F. G., 8, 14, 19 n. 10, 48, 79, 98
Balandier, G., 9, 20 n. 21
Banfield, E. C., 74, 107, 114
Barnes, J. A., 9
Barth, F., 8, 62
Berreman, G. D., 129
Bienen, H., 17
Blau, P., 8, 114
Boissevain, J., 79
Bond, Sir Robert, 71
'Boston States', emigration to, 23
Bowater Company, 40, 53
brokerage
   concept of, 48, 50, 79-80
   in Newfoundland, 25, 26, 32, 40, 45–6, 47, 49, 50, 61, 71, 73, 79, 80–1, 87, 97, 100, 110, 113, 114, 126
Brox, O., 22, 31, 70

Canadian Cancer Society, 56
Canadian Teachers' Federation, 56
Cat Harbour, 121–3 *passim*, 125
Catton, W., 9
Cicourel, A. V., 2
class, *see under* Focaltown, development of class in
'cognitive maps', *see under* myth, meanings and uses of
Cohen, Abner, 8, 9

Cohen, A. P., 74, 109, 114 n. 1, 122, 131 n. 3,
   and Comaroff, J. L., 80, 97
Cohen, D. L., 20 n. 17
Cohen, P. S., 12, 13, 20 n. 19, 21 n. 24
Commission of Government, 37 n. 4
'condensation symbols', 15
Confederation (with Canada), 12, 22, 23, 24, 29, 30, 31, 37 n. 4, 43, 57, 63, 66, 74 n. 12, 84, 130
Copes, P., 116
Costa Pinto, L. A., 21 n. 27, 97
Crosbie, J. C., 27, 28, 60 n. 6, 67, 114, 116, 126
Crysdale, S., 35
'cultural extension'
   and 'assertive marginality', 129–30
   examples of, 17, 70–1
   in Focaltown, *see under* People's Group
   meaning of, 15, 16, 39–40, 116, 128
   see also myth, management of
'cultural substitution'
   and 'assimilative marginality', 129–30
   examples, of, 17–18
   in Focaltown, *see under* Sophisticates' Group
   meaning of, 15, 16, 116
   see also myth, management of

Dahrendorf, R., 5
Dale Carnegie course, 108
Danzger, M. H., 20 n. 15
deference, 18, 41, 49, 51, 66, 75–6, 116–21, 123, 125, 127
Devons, E., 13
DeWitt, R. L., 35, 73, 104, 119
Dore, R. F., 73
Douglas, M., 20–1 n. 22

Doyle, J., 63
Durkheim, E., 13, 19 n. 4, 115
  Durkheimian tradition, 3, 13

Easton, D., 2, 5, 6–7, 8, 19, 20 n. 17
Eaton, Wayne (fictive), 40, 42, 43, 44, 53–4, 55, 56, 58, 59, 60, 61, 65, 68, 69, 70, 71, 72, 77, 89–90, 91–6 *passim*, 98, 100, 101, 106–8, 112, 120–1, 124; *see also* Sophisticates' Group
Edelman, M., 21 n. 23
Eidheim, H., 129
Epstein, A. L., 9
Evans, F. J., 41, 73, 85, 98, 116, 125, 126
Evans-Pritchard, E. E., 4, 5, 18 n. 2

Fallers, L., 8
Faris, J. C., 29, 66, 76, 84, 116, 121–3 *passim*, 125
Farrar, Donald (fictive), 54–5, 56, 58, 59, 60 n. 10, 65–6, 69, 72, 90, 92, 93, 100–1, 111, 112, 125; *see also* Sophisticates' Group
Feltham, J., 30, 43, 71, 116
Fishermen's Protective Union, 29–30
Focaltown
  Amalgamated School Board, 36, 41, 54, 56, 57, 68, 96, 125
  as consumer society, 23, 29, 32
  development of, 34, 43
  development of class in, 28–30, 32–3, 49, 63, 68
  as economic and service centre, 34
  family size in, 37 n. 5, 68
  image and identity of, 58–9, 123
  organisations in:
    Chamber of Commerce, 29, 31, 35, 36, 41, 48, 52, 56, 57, 62, 72, 77, 85, 87, 88, 90–2, 94–6, 102, 105, 111
    Lions Club, 29, 31, 35, 36, 41, 42, 48, 52, 56, 57, 59, 60 n. 13, 62, 67, 69, 84–5, 87, 88, 89, 90, 91, 102, 105, 106
    Town Council, 31, 35, 36, 37 n. 9, 45, 48, 49, 50, 52, 55, 56, 57, 59 n. 3, 70, 84–5, 86, 87, 89–90, 91, 94–5, 105, 120, 126–7
    other, 29, 31, 35, 36, 56–7, 60 n. 13, 84–5, 90–1, 102, 124
    see also under Herring Bay
  political legitimacy in, 1, 6, 9, 11, 12, 16, 18, 24–33, 44, 57–8, 73, 79, 101, 108, 114, 115–31; *see also* myth, management of, and sociopolitical change in Focaltown
  religions in:
    Anglicanism, 34–5, 67, 78
    Pentecostalism, 32–3, 34, 37 n. 7–8, 49, 67, 68–70, 74 n. 7, 78, 102–5, 113
    Salvationism, 34–5, 37 n. 7, 54, 67, 78
    United Church (Methodism), 34–5, 37 n. 7, 42, 67, 78
  unemployment in, 22, 32, 36 n. 1, 68, 103
Focaltown News, 60, 62, 94–6, 98
'foolish leader', 80, 85, 122
Fortes, M. and Evans-Pritchard, E. E., 3
Foster, G., 17, 79
Frankenberg, R., 85
Freeman, M. M. R., 71

Glaser, B. and Strauss, A. L., 2
Glass, R., 129
Glickman, H., 17
Gluckman, M., 3, 20 n. 22
Goffman, E., 20 n. 22, 68, 129
Goody, J., 20 n. 22
Gouldner, A., 11
Gwyn, R., 24, 63, 66, 70, 75, 113, 116

Habenstein, R. W., 129
Harris, L., 67
Herrick, C. S., 37 n. 2, 70
Herring Bay
  'Action-for-Joey' Committee, 48, 67, 70, 105; *see also* Liberal Party of Newfoundland and Labrador, leadership of
  Consolidated School Board, 54, 69, 100
  District Liberal Association, *see under* Liberal Party of Newfoundland and Labrador, in Herring Bay
  Economic Development Association, 31, 35, 36, 49, 56, 57, 62, 72, 88, 91–3, 97, 100–1, 112, 124, 128
Hickman, T. Alex, 28
Historical Statistics of Newfoundland and Labrador, 74 n. 6
Hobbes, T., 6, 19 n. 5
Hodgkin, T., 18

144 The management of myths

Homans, G. C., 3, 19 n. 6
Horwood, H., 24, 66, 98
Hoselitz, B. F., 17

identity management, strategies of, 129–31
'interactionist' sociology, 10, 19 n. 10
intermediate technology, 71
Iverson, N. and Matthews, D. R., 26, 51, 70

Jacob, P. E. and Teune, H., 38
Job Brothers, 72

Kavadias, G., 17, 18
Kavanagh, D., 117
Kirk, G. S., 13
Klapp, O. E., 129
Kuper, A., 8, 9

Laponce, J. A., 21 n. 23
Leach, E. R., 8, 13, 14, 20 n. 11
leadership, *see under* Focaltown, political legitimacy in; *and* People's Group; *and* Sophisticates' Group
legitimacy
  'by association, or extension', 44, 45, 75, 113
  'by incumbency', 44, 113
  defined, 11, 115
  and models of politics, 2–11, 115
  as political resource, 2, 9, 11, 12, 16, 20 n. 17, 25, 58, 97, 101, 112, 129
  and power, 6–7, 9, 20 n. 12, 127
  strategic acquisition of, *see under* myth, management of
  see also Focaltown, political legitimacy in
the 'Legitimisers', 37 n. 10, 60 n. 11, 72, 83–7, 89–96, 108, 122, 127
Lester, Stan (fictive), 40, 47–51, 55, 62, 65–6, 67, 69–70, 71, 72, 76, 77, 78, 79–83, 86, 87, 96, 97, 100–1, 104, 105, 110–11, 113, 120, 126; *see also* People's Group
LeVine, R. A., 51
Lévi-Strauss, C., 13, 115
Liberal Party of Canada, 27, 37 n. 3, 48, 65, 105, 110
Liberal Party of Newfoundland and Labrador
  in Herring Bay, 35, 46, 48, 69, 74 n. 8, 100, 105, 110

leadership of, 27–8, 37 n. 4, 47, 48, 56, 58, 60 n. 6, 62, 64, 67, 83, 84, 104, 114 n.
local associations of, 28, 45, 61–2, 105
Lienhardt, G., 20 n. 22
Lodge, T., 37 n. 4, 42
The Loyal Liberal, 74 n. 2
Lush, Ivan (fictive), 55–6, 57, 58, 69, 77, 78, 92, 112, 127; *see also* Sophisticates' Group

McLintock, A. H., 42, 131 n. 2
Malinowski, B., 13, 14, 16
Maranda, P., 14
March, J., 20 n. 15
Marriott, M., 17
Martin family (fictive), 40–4, 48, 53, 96, 100, 101
  Arthur, 40–4, 48, 50, 51, 55, 58, 71, 76, 78, 82, 84, 86–7, 90, 113; *see also* People's Group
  Edward, 40–4, 51, 53, 56, 60 n. 8, 61, 67, 112, 123
  Frank, 41, 69–70
  Jacob, 40, 41, 51, 60 n. 8
  James, 41, 71, 92
Marx, K., 115
Matthews, D. R., 26, 41, 51, 70
Mayer, A. C., 79
Miller, J. D. B., 19 n. 10
Mitchell, W. C., 5
Murphy, R. F., 9
myth
  management of, 15–18, 36, 38, 45, 51, 57, 115–16, 127
  and socio-political change in Focaltown, 15–17, 18, 38, 39–40, 57, 61–74 *passim*, 75, 97, 101, 116, 127–9, 130
  meanings and uses of, 12–14, 16, 20 ns. 18–21, 24, 115
  see also 'cultural extension'; *and* 'cultural substitution'

Nadel, S. F., 3, 20 n. 22
Nemec, T., 29, 121, 131 n. 1
Nettler, G., 9
Newfoundland Ranger Force, 55, 93
Newfoundland Royal Commission, 40, 125
Newfoundland, Royal Commission on Economic State and Prospects of, 70

Newfoundland Teachers' Association, 56, 69
Noel, S. J. R., 24, 66, 74 n. 3, 118, 119
Nyerere, J., 17

Ontario, emigration to, 23

Paine, R. P. B., 61, 79, 97–8
Parsons, T., 5–6, 19, 20 n. 22
patronage, 25, 32, 33, 45–6, 50, 61, 62, 71, 79, 80, 100–1, 110, 114, 125–6, 128
'People's Group'
  characteristics and strategies of, 36, 38, 39–51, 52, 59, 78–88, 120, 122
  individualism, 42, 48, 50, 52, 75, 76, 77, 96, 111
  organisational membership, 39, 41, 48, 56, 122
  and 'Legitimisers', 37 n. 10, 85–6
  myths, nature of, 38, 39–40, 61, 63, 70, 73, 97, 101, 112–14, 126, *see also* 'cultural extension'
  and Pentecostalists, 37 n. 8, 67, 102–5, 113
  see also Lester, Stan; *and* Martin family; *and* Rodgers, Thomas; *and* peripheral activism
peripheral activism
  of Legitimisers, 85, 92
  in People's Group, 41, 102–5, 108, 113
  in Sophisticates' Group, 52, 77, 102, 106–10
Perlin, A. B., 70
Perlin, G. C., 24, 51, 61, 66, 67, 70, 74 n. 2, 113, 121
Political Systems of Highland Burma, 8
politics
  defined, 11, 129–31
  models of, and legitimacy, 2–11
  political legitimation, *see under* myth, management of
  power, 4, 128
    in Focaltown, 11, 41–2, 50, 128; *see also* Focaltown, political legitimacy in
    interactional nature of, 10–11
    and legitimacy, 6–7, 9, 20 n. 12, 127–9
    as political resource, 9
  'processual' analysis, 7–11
Progressive Conservative Party of Newfoundland and Labrador, 27, 28, 35, 37 n. 3, 57, 58, 60 n. 14, 64, 66, 112, 127

Prowse, D. W., 43, 131 n. 2

Radcliffe-Brown, A. R., 3, 4, 5, 7, 20 n. 22
resettlement programme, 17, 25–7, 70
'Responsible Government', 37 n. 4, 66
ritual, 13, 15, 20 n. 22, 24, 52, 62, 93, 114, 115, 116
Rodgers, Thomas (fictive), 40, 44–6, 48, 50, 51, 65–6, 75, 82, 84, 86, 96, 105, 113; *see also* People's Group
Rowe, F. W., 74 n. 5

St. John's, merchants of, 23, 24, 28, 43
segmentary lineage systems, 3, 4
Shaheen, J., 63
Sharrock, W. W., 5
Silverman, S. F., 79, 114
Skolnik, M., 26
Smallwood, J. R., 17, 22, 24–5, 27–8, 30, 37 n. 3, 39, 40, 44–5, 46, 47–51, 58, 60, 61–2, 63, 64–6, 67, 70, 71, 73, 74, 75, 80–1, 82–3, 84, 86, 101, 102, 104, 110, 111–12, 114 n. 3
Smallwoodism, 25, 38, 61, 62, 63, 66, 105
Smallwood Liberalism, 50
Smith,, Marjorie, 42, 66, 116
Smith, M. G., 4, 5
'Sophisticates' Group'
  characteristics and strategies of, 33, 36, 39, 44, 49, 51, 52–9, 62, 88, 97, 120, 122
  organisational activity, 35, 42, 49, 52, 55–7, 62, 72–3, 75, 76, 77, 87, 88–97, 102, 111, 114, 122, 127–8
  and 'Legitimisers', 37 n. 10, 85, 89–96
  myths, nature of, 18, 38, 39, 43, 52, 58, 61, 62–3, 73, 97, 101, 106–10, 112, 124, 126; *see also* 'cultural substitution'
  and Pentecostalists, 37 n. 8
  see also Eaton, Wayne; *and* Farrar, Donald; *and* Lush, Ivan; *and* Whiteway, John; *and* peripheral activism
Sperber, D., 14
Squires, Sir Richard, 71
Stiles, R. G., 29, 83, 116, 121
structural functionalism, 2–7, 10, 19 n. 4
Swartz, M., 9
Swartz, M., Turner, V. W., and Tuden, A., 9
Szwed, J., 119

Thoms, J. R., 70, 74 n. 11
Trudeau, P., 27
Turner, V. W., 8, 21 n. 22

Wadel, C., 22, 26, 31, 37 n. 6, 70, 98, 103, 116, 129
Wagner, G., 19 n. 3
Weber, M., 3, 5, 6, 7, 19 n. 5, 20 n. 17
Wells, C., 27
The Western Star, 74 n. 9

White, D. M., 20 n. 15
Whiteway, John (fictive), 55–6, 58, 72, 77, 90, 92, 93, 112, 125; *see also* Sophisticates' Group
Whiteway, Sir William, 71
Willener, A., 21 n. 26
Wilson, B. R., 102, 103
Wolf, E., 79
Worsley, P. M., 9, 11, 15, 20 n. 17, 21 n. 26, 51